KID OF THE KING

LONG TIME LOST, FOREVER FOUND

THE TRUE LIFE STORY OF ELAINE ELIZABETH "LIZ" PRESLEY

BY

LIZ PRESLEY

KID OF THE KING

ISBN : 978-1-7365062-0-2

Editor: Dr. Billie J. Minton

PREFACE

I desired to tell the story of my life. It amazed me to discover that I am the daughter of Elvis and Priscilla Presley.

I needed for my family to see the life that I lived while on the road in discovering who I truly am. It has been a long and difficult journey.

Writing this book has definitely been therapeutic in helping me heal from my past. Although I grew up in the wrong family, I do not have any regrets of the life that I have lived. My past experiences have allowed me to have a strong sense of survival and has taught me that giving up is never a choice.

Nothing means more to me than the love and protection of my family.

DEDICATION

I dedicate this book to the following:

God, my Almighty Father in Heaven, who kept me safe and guides my path.

My mother, Mildred Hynard, for giving me love, care, protection, and for keeping me safe up until I was thirteen years old.

My Nanna, in England, who was the first to tell me that I was a "special child." She loved and cared for me. Her messages gave me the wisdom to discover where I came from.

My father, Elvis Presley, who brought me home in 2013 by some incredible, spiritual means. I feel his constant love and protection every day.

My mother, Priscilla Presley, who never once pushed me away when I came home to Graceland. I feel her love every day in my heart.

My sister, Lisa Marie, who shows me compassion and who joined me in a song which honors our family entitled, "Graceland Anthem."

My daughter, who gave me a family purpose in my life. Raising a wonderful, loving daughter is the biggest accomplishment I will ever achieve.

My nephew, Benjamin, whose memory remains in my heart daily.

My friends and family, who stood by me through my incredible journey of coming home to Graceland.

ACKNOWLEDGMENTS

I would like to thank all of the people throughout my life that helped and assisted me on my long and arduous journey home. There were many winding roads, from being a child that became lost after my father's death, to a soul that would not stop searching for my destiny. Throughout my voyage, I traveled in darkness, but I followed my heart and believed in the goal that one day I would find what I was searching for.

There are far too many people to thank and name here, but I earnestly applaud you all. I am eternally grateful to each and every one of you:

- My mother, who raised me, Mildred Valerie Hynard, whom I loved and adored. She loved and adored me and kept me safe during my early childhood years up until age thirteen.

- The Boyles Court, Brentwood, England, where I was able to find structure and peace for two years.

- The Trust House Forte Hotel group, London, who looked after me for seven years until I moved to America, the same hotel group that my father, Elvis Presley, was in negotiations with during the same time I was living there.

- My father, Elvis Presley, who brought me home and is forever here in spirit.

- My devoted daughter, whom I love dearly and with all my heart.

- Victoria and Leo, who supported and sponsored me into America.

- Max and Haley, who helped me when I needed help.

- My friend, Grant, who also greatly supported me.

- Jetta, who was a great friend to me.

- Jayne and Barbara, who provided me with a mother figure and who freely gave their limitless love and guidance.

- Dr. Billie J. Minton, my Editor, who spent countless hours with me ensuring this book was authentic and professional.

- Irene Leland, whom I am so grateful to for writing the original manuscript of my life story.

- Special thanks to Aaron Pacentine for the cover photo.

- My sister, Lisa Marie Presley.

- My mother, Priscilla Presley, who shows me love and care.

- My cousins, who were there for me while I was coming home.

- Last, but not least, all my many friends and fans who continue to support me, no matter what!

FOREWORD

The first time I met with Liz Presley, I said, "Liz, you look and sound like your true DNA, dear. We all do, and your family DNA has revealed itself in you."

At that moment, Liz knew exactly what I meant. She is such a kind and genuine soul who searches for truth and has the uncanny ability to make a connection with everyone she meets.

When Liz Presley first asked me to help support her in the writing of her autobiography, I was involved in many active, ongoing, and developing projects. I was unsure whether or not I would able to devote the time necessary, but when Liz looked at me with her sincere, piercing green eyes and said, "I need my true life story to be in the care of your hands," I could not refuse and I asked Liz to send me her transcript. There are few things more satisfying than knowing someone I admire recognizes and enjoys my work. Working with Liz has been an honor.

When I first reviewed Liz's book, I noticed how the pages were written with such a soft, heartfelt delivery, but also conveyed such unwavering strength. Her life story evokes feelings, stirs memories, and provokes thoughts of the past, present, and future. Liz's story blew my mind and her honesty had me wearing an enormous smile.

Although it is apparent that Liz was lost and searching for something most all of her life, she is an overachiever and a survivor. I enjoyed the part of her book which revealed how she gained immediate confidence for the first time in her life after she came home to Graceland in 2013. No matter what Liz endured in her life, she always maintained happiness within herself and in those around her.

Liz is a very successful business woman, but the love that she shares with so many family members and friends is the deepest well that she draws upon. Her endless smiles show it. Giving birth to things others can enjoy always makes her happy. Creating anything gets her excited. She never forgets about the "simple things" in life, either.

Liz Presley has such an idyllic personality and takes the time to help others in need. She feels the need to put an extra spring in someone's step. Her sweet and thoughtful nature will warm your heart.

Liz is a very spiritual person of strong intellect, yet embraces a keen business acumen. Such attributes are rare and are an intriguing combination. She is such an intelligent guiding force. Liz is both a gift and a blessing to everyone in her life. She has spent so much time searching in her life, but I doubt that she ever noticed the years for the minutes. It seemed like Liz had a moment when everything came to fruition on May 6, 2013. I believe she may have staggered under the hugeness of the realization of discovering who her biological parents were. Fortunately for Liz, life has brought her many moments of joy to balance out the painful years of searching.

Each day is a great opportunity for Liz to live her life honoring her father's legacy. She has great talent herself and it is second only to her character and humility.

I invite you, dear reader, to sit back, relax, and hang on tight while reading the true adventures of Liz Presley's life. I hope you enjoy her true life story as much as I did.

Dr. Billie J. Minton,

Author of Blue Ridge Moments and

Blue Ridge Tenderpups children series

Kingsport, Tennessee

TABLE OF CONTENTS

TRUTH AWAKENS

On May 6, 2013, my life was so dramatically impacted that I knew it would be changed forever. I was suddenly no longer a fifty-four year old divorced, single parent, living a quiet life in my modest home in Wales, England. Instead, it was on this particularly chilly, rainy afternoon that I sat down on my couch to make a decision. A similar decision I made when I was seventeen years old, when I had to decide whether to study business or take music lessons. This decision, however, was much more serious.

I had been lost for many years and was searching. My soul was unsure what it was searching for and I was tired. I had been singing as "Elainee" for two years. I decided to pray to God and let Him know that I would no longer be searching for whatever it was that I was trying to find. I decided I would simply settle-in and be "Elainee". I chose to make my fans my family because I did not feel like I belonged anywhere. At that moment, my life flashed before me. I saw Elvis Presley. All of the pieces of my life came together. I suddenly felt found and instantly confident. Some type of miracle had happened. Before the flashbacks from my childhood until then, I said to myself, with my dog Buffy by my side, "Oh my goodness, that's what I have been looking for."

From the time I turned away from Elvis Presley when I was seventeen until that moment, I realized that he was most likely my father. I moved forward from that amazing moment with my new life. Knowing who I was gave me a strong sense of confidence. I now realized who my biological father was and it all made sense, based on "the whispers" that had surrounded me as a child. However, I knew that I had to scientifically prove to the rest of the world exactly what I discovered in my heart. As you read my story, you will learn the full extent of what happened to me growing up as a lost child.

An Unusual Beginning

Growing up, I believed I was born December 11, 1959 in Little Clacton On Sea in Essex, England to my parents, Dennis Mower and Mildred Hynard, and given the name David Mower. My father was a staunch military man and was enlisted and on active duty in the army when I was born. He was serving in Germany while, at the same time, my mother was working as an army volunteer worker for the Red Cross when I was conceived.

From the beginning, I was not an ordinary newborn. I was born both a girl and a boy, what doctors described as intersexed; a combination of having what are considered both male and female genitalia. The medical team determined that early gender assignment would be important for my future emotional well-being, but the choice for my parents was not easy. It seemed I was more preternaturally a little girl; mentally, emotionally, and physiologically, but it wouldn't be until many years later that I would choose to become my true self; Elaine Elizabeth Presley.

I grew-up in a small shack in Marks Tey, not far from the town of Colchester, the hub of the army barracks in England. We lived in an extremely primitive environment and our standard of living was meager and exceedingly limited. Our home had no electricity and no indoor plumbing. My mother was forced to boil our water for safe drinking and for heating my bath water when I was bathed in an old English

3

metal tub. Of course our family did not have the luxury of buying diapers. Rather, I was wrapped in what we in England called "nappies," which are simply cloth diapers that were hand washed and hung outside on a makeshift clothesline to dry.

I was a happy child and I did not feel as if I lacked the basic necessities in my life, despite having to use an outhouse that was located approximately twenty yards away from our little house, which could be perilous at times. I can still remember a late night visit to the outhouse on a freezing evening when I tripped on an old rake and the handle flew up, hitting and bruising my head. I ultimately used the facility and stumbled back to bed only to be doted on by my loving mother in the morning.

I was told that I was a very handsome young man. I was absolutely adored by my mother and I had a few friends, the majority of which were girls. I was the envy of other boys. It was said that I was not like the rowdy boys in our neighborhood. The girls were seemingly drawn to my sensitiveness and empathy, but also to my sense of humor and fun loving nature.

Throughout my formative years and older, women were in and out of my life until I eventually married, but I treasured the loving companionship with each relationship I enjoyed. I learned that I was naturally a good listener. It seemed odd, however, that I could be so different from the rest of my family.

My father, who was a stern disciplinarian and uncommonly uncommunicative, could also be incredibly cruel. I often wondered how I could have developed into a boy who was deemed good natured and loving, but who shared nothing in common with the rest of the family.

My father was openly unaccepting of my intersex biology and was fiercely determined to shape me into my becoming what his idea of what a man should aspire to be. My father would task me incredible labor intensive jobs around our house and surrounding property; "man's work," my father would say. It was my father's resolve to groom me into becoming a man so not be embarrassed or shamed in our small village by his son. The difference between the man my father wanted me to become and to the woman I now am was more apparent and pronounced as I grew older. While I attribute most of my positive qualities to my mother, I still felt somehow disconnected from the one person who I knew loved me most in this world, my mother.

I grew-up with two siblings in our small home; my brother Jack and my sister Daisy, with whom I had little or no connection, even though at times, we did play together. Jack and Daisy shared a special kinship with one another to which I was excluded. I could not understand why, as their brother, I was not invited into their childhood fun and not share in their adolescent secrets, all the while feeling no intrinsic fraternal bond with either.

Between the ever increasing ridicule of my father and feeling the distance between myself, my brother, and my sister, the only positive influence being my mother in my life, was perhaps only foreshadowing what I would later learn that would explain what I was feeling. The ultimate realization would change the course of my life forever.

It was sometimes a struggle living in poverty and grappling with my strained family relationships; my father's heavy hand and the stark division between myself and my siblings. It was my mother who was my constant, who was always there to comfort and stand by me. Her steadfast devotion to me was unparalleled and she never failed to demonstrate to me that I was loved beyond measure, and she taught me to believe in myself. I will be always be grateful to my loving mother.

MOVING ON UP

I was almost five years old when we moved out of our small house to a newly built home in the village of Coggeshall, approximately ten miles away from Colchester. Our new three bedroom, heated house, complete with indoor plumbing, sat next to rich farmland where my father worked, farming weekdays in exchange for rent, and worked as a logger on the weekends. Despite my father's lack of affection for me, he was a hard worker and tried his best to provide for our family. I respect my father's dogged determination to give his family shelter and to put food on our table.

Jack and I helped my father work on the farm. I quickly learned how to lift and stack bales of hay and load them onto a trailer hitched to a tractor that my brother would drive. I was not allowed to drive the tractor or do certain dangerous jobs. Jack and I were tasked to go into the woods two miles away. Jack would saw down trees into large chunks, for which they would lie for one year to dry out. Then, later, it was my job to chop the wood into smaller pieces. We were both responsible for bagging wood into fertilizer bags, and hauling them onto the trailer to be delivered to customers in the surrounding villages. I suppose my slight frame and delicate nature was what made my father believe that I could not have possibly worked as hard as my brother, and only Jack would receive pay for our day's work, which was not uncommon in our household for any paying jobs we undertook.

Despite being slighted by my father, I was always eager to work and I looked forward to pea and potato picking season when I was allowed to work on other farms. I enjoyed the feel of the potatoes in my hand and packing the potatoes in large brown sacks, but the peas were handled much differently. The peas were placed into metal buckets, only the best peas being tediously selected, before the peas were poured into mesh sacks. When the currants were in season, I liked to pick through them and arrange them into compartments on trays. It was ultimately satisfying for me to do this kind of work. I was proud that I could contribute to the family and aid my father in earning money.

For fun, I found great pleasure in hunting for wild strawberries, raspberries, gooseberries, and blackberries in the surrounding fields. It was wonderful to see how happy it would make my mother to see me walk through the door carrying sacks of berries. She would wash and bake them into fruit pies or delicious crumble cakes. I would sometimes play in the river near Coggeshall and catch eels. The hotel in town would pay me a farthing or two, which at the time, was a lot of money to me since I had none of my own. As I grew a little older, I washed cars and later had my own paper route. I can thank my father for helping me develop a strong work ethic.

I first attended St. Peter's Primary School and was later enrolled in Honeywood High School. I eventually transferred to Alec Hunter High School. I was a quiet and shy student and was often bullied, earning the nickname "Flea Bags" because my clothes were cheap and shoddy. I was too sensitive to defend myself, but thankfully I had the natural ability to make my classmates laugh and was able to make a few friends. As I grew more comfortable within myself, girls seemed to gravitate towards me, telling me that I was different. I was told that I had an uncanny way of understanding, empathizing, and bringing comfort to them.

I often had trouble paying for school lunches and I would secretly rummage in trash bins for unused lunch tickets. My mother had begun to drink and her alcoholism had taken over. She was using our household money to buy alcohol, and on most days there was nothing left for which to buy groceries. On a good day, my mother might manage to make me a sandwich, sometimes a banana sandwich or peanut butter with grape or strawberry jam sandwich. On other days, I might find a butter and sugar sandwich, or a cheese and pickle sandwich in my paper sack. My mother was trying her best, under the circumstances, and I loved her for it. I understood her pain.

I walked to and from school. One unlucky morning while attending St. Peter's Primary School, I was struck by a white van while crossing the street. I was catapulted several feet into the air and landed on the side of the road, bleeding and unconscious. When I awakened, I found that I was unable to walk. The driver of the van carried me to my home and left me in the care of my distressed mother. It was almost a month before I was able to walk again, all the while the man who hit me visited often and brought me gifts.

My father's disdainful and dismissive treatment of me continued and progressively grew worse. His behavior began to take its toll on my mother. It agonized her to see how I was treated differently from both my brother and sister, and she was doing her best to see that I was treated fairly.

My mother worked hard and was committed to keeping her family happy and her home running as smoothly as possible, but we shared a special bond, separate from my siblings. My mother would take me with her to the grocery store, whether it was our walking one mile to the bus stop, or my riding in the basket of her pushbike, it was our special time together. On several occasions, my mother would take me with her to the pub while she drank a cocktail or two. It was easy for me to see that my mother was beautiful and was always attracting a great deal of attention from the men around her.

Having to witness my father belittle me daily was devastating for my mother. Of course, my mother loved all of her children, but I believe she felt she needed to protect and love me more to make up for all of my obvious weaknesses and for the lack of love and attention from my father. I was stunned to hear part of an argument between my parents, during which my father was berating my mother, and I thought I heard him claim that I was not his son. I asked myself, "Did he really say that?"

A DOWNWARD SPIRAL

The tyranny of my father endured and the arguments between my parents increased. The dissolution of their marriage seemed imminent and my mother began to drink more heavily. I was losing my only ally in the family and my one true friend to alcohol. In the meantime, my father was relentless in his pursuit to shame me for not being "all boy," and perhaps, if I heard correctly, for possibly not being his son. The constant pressure to perform was enormous. My father was determined to turn me into his idea of what a boy should be; a farm hand, a football player, and an army recruit. He was a formidable force and unyielding in his attempts to bring out the "male" in me. He became obsessive in his resolve and coerced me into having surgery to correct my genitals. The surgical intervention was to masculinize my genitalia to be more like those of a typical male. My father lied to me by telling me that if did not have the surgery, I would contract cancer.

The delicate surgery was paid for by our English government and did not burden my family financially. I spent three long months recuperating in the hospital, until the surgeons determined that there were complications and I had to undergo another surgical procedure. It was devastating. I spent an additional three weeks in the critical care unit. My rehabilitation period was excruciating. I was forced to take Epsom salt baths which were extremely painful. I did not fully understand the extent of how my body was changing, but I did know it was purely to satisfy my father. I was emotionally and physically experiencing so much pain. A side effect of the surgery was that my testosterone levels were heightened and caused periodic episodes of shaking, confusion, and depression. It is a memory I would like to forget.

I looked to my mother for comfort, but in addition to her abusing alcohol, she had become addicted to prescription pills and was emotionally unavailable. As much as I loved my mother, I resented the fact that she would not hold my father accountable for his actions; being a substandard husband and an unaccepting father. It seemed my mother simply did not have the courage to leave him, though, with her beauty, she could have had any number of suitors.

I eventually fully healed and life returned to normal. I suppose my surgery appeased my father, but he remained distant. There was no real change in our lifestyle and because since it was the way of life I knew, I was content. It wasn't until later that my father's domineering and overbearing character would be an issue and would cause disastrous consequences.

My mother's health began to decline, physically and mentally. She became emotionally unstable due to her drug use. My mother became obsessively compulsive and her behavior odd, turning lights on and off without reason, chattering nonsensically, rapidly blinking her eyes, and blindly roaming about the house. Physiologically, my mother's body would twitch involuntarily and it was frightening. We tried to compel our mother to allow us to take her to the hospital, but she was adamant that would not relent and refused treatment.

I was extremely concerned for my mother's health, but I felt powerless to help her. It did not make matters better that my mother drank outside our home, frequenting the village pubs of Coggeshall and Colchester. I often came home to an inebriated mother, too drunk to function. I loved my mother and would never want disparage her by admitting that I was often embarrassed to see my mother sitting off kilter on a town bench, her arms twitching, eyes blinking, and talking to herself. I would run to her side and implore her to come home with me, but rarely was I successful. It pains me to think of who my mother once was, loving and nurturing, to the woman she ultimately became, a mere shadow of her former self. I blame my father.

CLOWNING AROUND TOWN

I was fortunate to make two very good childhood friends, William and Patrick. The three of us together were a mischievous crew and the village of Coggeshall was our playground, and was subject to our spirited, but innocent antics. I became the leader of our little gang. I was fascinated that one of the Coggeshall residents collected miniature concrete gnomes. Each gnome depicted an activity; fishing in a tiny bird bath, daydreaming on their backs, petting a cat, and some happy, some sad, others clapping and dancing. They were marvelous to me.

In the mind of this pre-teen, I concocted a prank that would be mutually harmless, but also daring; mysterious gnome transportation. The plan was for our threesome to relocate the neighbor's gnomes and displace them to the home of another neighbor, placing each gnome in the exact position as originally positioned from their original home place. The confusion that ensued was fun to watch from afar, and we laughed until our bellies ached.

The success of our chicanery only bolstered our resolve to repeat our trickery. There were no clues we left behind and the rumors swirled throughout the community. No one knew, nor would have suspected, four young boys from another village to have been so clever. A month later, we decided to orchestrate another plan to displace the now infamous Coggeshall gnome family.

Our rogue youth troupe crept into the neighbor's garden, once again. We readied ourselves for a repeat performance of what we called, "gnome transportation." Unfortunately, the homeowners were ready. With beaming flashlights and raised rakes, we were taken by surprise and immediately chased away. It was our bad luck that we were recognized as the boys who were from the neighboring village. We were identified and the confrontation between the homeowners and my parents earned me a severe clap to the ears, a ringing that I could hear for days afterward.

It might have been believed by some that Patrick, William, and myself would have tempered our lust for fun and adventure after our gnome debacle, but not so. We simply limited ourselves to less risky pursuits. We found adventure in running about after dark, visiting various church grounds. We would don ourselves with our mother's best sheets and hide behind the many large gravestones. We would leap from our hidden positions, hoping to frighten any passersby. It is not to say that we did not have great fun in such innocent play, but I did not escape several more claps to the side of my head from my father, not that it was not undeserved. As stern as my father was, I was never beaten for any infractions that he didn't deem as simple "boy's play." For that, I am grateful, though I would later disappoint him.

Celebrating Guy Fawkes Day was always an anticipated holiday for me and my family. In England, Guy Fawkes was a co-conspirator in a plot to assassinate King James I who was determined to incinerate the Palace of Westminster. The plan was foiled and Guy Fawkes was tried, found guilty, and burned at the stake. In effigy, Fawkes is burned every year, accompanied by fireworks and cheer. Our Guy Fawkes Day might be similar in celebration to Halloween in the United States, but with certainly different roots, but no less fun.

Anyone chosen to portray Guy Fawkes had to sit perfectly still while being pulled around the village in a wagon begging for pennies. We were trying to prove, after all, that Guy Fawkes was dead; a hated traitor to England. If the sitting Guy Fawkes individual was in the wagon was seen making any movement whatsoever, you were deemed a fake and rejected; no pennies given. As a lark, and a way to distance myself from my family, my friends and I decided to designate me as our own Guy Fawkes, without parental supervision, and collect our own pennies.

We knocked on the front door of the first home we visited and, when the door opened, the homeowner studied me as I was dressed in my Guy Fawkes garb. I sat as still as humanly possible and I thought I was doing a pretty good job. Before my friends had a moment to say, "Penny for the Guy," the man pulled out a knife and lunged towards me. The man yelled, "What is this? Is this the real Guy Fawkes or a fake?" In a flash, I was out of the wheelbarrow and running, with my friends not far behind me. I laugh about it today, and I often wonder if that man has a chuckle or two himself, when he remembers that particular Guy Fawkes Day.

SIMPLE JOYS

As I grew older and gradually abandoned my adolescent tendencies and began to seek-out more pleasurable mature interests, intimate relationships became more of a focus to me. As a child of six or seven years of age, I was curious, confused, and I innocently experimented with Alexander. I felt more like a girl than a boy, and our brief romance entailed having our first kiss of life in the cornfields. I did not enjoy this first kiss with Alexander, therefore, it did not happen again.

When I was about eleven years old, I became enraptured with Paula. We would go on long walks holding hands, and hang-out just about everywhere in Coggeshall. When Paula did not show up for several days, I sadly realized our brief romance was over. Next, at approximately age thirteen, I met Sarah in Braintree. She was from an upper crust family and liked me in spite of my outward appearance. While feeling embarrassed wearing old, ragged trousers, Sarah picked me up and sat me on a park bench. She kissed me and we instantly became enthralled with these simple romantic joys. The two of us found lightheartedness in sitting on the park bench just talking and kissing. I suddenly became inspired with the idea that if I bleached my trousers that they would look newer, cleaner, and impress Sarah. I poured so much bleach on my trousers that they turned white and began to fall apart during my next innocent encounter with Sarah. After that day, Sarah and I did not see each other again.

At the same time my interest in girls had peaked, I realized that I had an infatuation for music. I adored listening and singing songs ever since I was a young child. I affectionately remember when my mother bought me my first 45 record, "Old McDonald Had a Farm," and then later, my second treasure, "Living Doll." Since my sister, Daisy, was the one who had a record player in her bedroom, I would bound into her room when she was out of the house and immerse myself in the repetitive sounds that never failed to captivate me. I indulged myself in playing Daisy's records, too, as well as a few of my mother's. I loved to sing along with every note and never wanted any song to end. I especially enjoyed switching a 45 record speed to a higher speed of 78 and I would sing in a higher pitch. I felt like I was rockin' with the sound on a faster track.

A favorite pastime of mine was to hang-out with the local tramp who lived by the tree in the nearby park. My friends and I would bring him food. The tramp relished in telling us his real life stories from the days of being a soldier and how it was that he became shell shocked. We also found pleasure in keeping company with the hippies who took up shelter in the abandoned homes in the village. We enjoyed the thrill of being around the friendly dissenters who captivated us with their guitar playing and musical routines while ranting against war and advocating for peace.

One time, I was so proud and filled up with expressive and creative sounds that I bounced downstairs in musical delight and put on my own little show, singing and dancing for Mildred and Dennis. I reenacted a slow song to a faster rock 'n' roll pace, but before I got a chance for my splash ending, Dennis cut me off, saying, "Stop it, you're not original. Elvis Presley sings and dances like that. You and Elvis can't sing, and neither of you will last very long!"

I had not given much attention to Elvis at that time, aside from hearing his name spoken. Later, when I caught a glimpse of Elvis doing his act on television, I asked my mother a question; "Hey Mum, how come someone can do the same thing as me? How will I ever be original?" I danced like Elvis and had a natural vibrato in my voice delivery that sounded just like Elvis. My mother simply smiled.

There were times that I felt confused and frustrated. I felt as if my voice was somehow wrong. I would walk down the street trying to sing out in another way that was different. Every time I tried, the altered voice was definitely not mine and certainly did not feel right. It was forced and not natural. As a result, Dennis refused to let me have music lessons. I desperately wanted to be musically trained. I would watch through a little window of the door at school as my classmates learned music, playing piano, strumming guitar, and learning how to play many other wonderful instruments. This made me feel extremely sad and left out.

OUT AND BEYOND

While living under the problematic circumstances of my mother's demise, and the ongoing fighting between Dennis and my mother, I broke out and ran away to Great Yarmouth On The Sea one summer when I was thirteen years old. Great Yarmouth On The Sea was a popular seaside town. I had spent weekends there before with my friends and I knew it well. I was very familiar with the surroundings. It was known for its amusement park, and that is where I was able to find work. I sold tickets and operated various rides. I basically roughed it by hanging-out on the streets and by finding a sleeping spot on the beach or at a hotel.

I received a lot of pleasure by entering a singing competition at a local hotel. I sang an original children's song that I had written entitled, "I Love You." I won second place. I really got a kick out of entertaining and singing rock 'n' roll songs for tourists at hotels.

All in all, I found a satisfying niche in being a "Teddy Boy". This was definitely the thing at that time. It was an animate part of an evolution, raised out of the depression, and the invention of Rock N' Roll in the 50's and 60's.

Being a Teddy Boy was one of five essential components of this phenomenon:

Rockers: These were hard core Rock N' Roll bikers. They wore leather jackets and blue jeans. Some of them had tattoos.

Teddy Boys: They were Rock N' Rollers, wore blue suede shoes, had fashioned hair and clothes of the Fifties. Some of them had tattoos.

Mods: These guys were funky Scooters, looking modern in their suits. They wore long parker coats, nice shoes, and had professional haircuts.

Punk Rockers: They were lovers of hard punk rock music. These dudes had safety pins in their nose, mouth, and ears. They definitely had tattoos. They had multi colored hair that stood up and they flaunted colorful clothing.

Skin Heads: They had shaved heads, and these dudes wore blue jeans which were turned up at the bottom, and black steel toe boots. They carried flick knives, and were hard and tough. They were known as Head Bangers.

I discovered that I perfectly fitted the image of the "Teddy Boy."

Whether I was on the street, roaming around, hanging out on the beach, playing the penny arcade, or going to the rock 'n' roll dance clubs, I had a natural, suave way of engaging with folks of all kinds. In teddy boy antics, I would smoothly pull out my comb from my back pocket, giving a straight boy look, curling my lip, and sleekly combing my hair.

At the end of that summer, I returned to my home in Coggeshall and my school life at Honeywood. On the weekends, and some weeknights,

I reluctantly became a part of the Army Cadets in the town of Braintree, west of Coggeshall, about eight miles away. Whether it was for four hours in the late afternoon and evening, or for a whole day, it was a disciplinary routine on which Dennis insisted I participate in real hard physical training and constant body testing. I would either take the bus or ride the bike back and forth. This became an ongoing strain for me along with the other elements of my environmental issues. Nevertheless, I prevailed.

Unbeknownst to Jack and me at the time, Dennis had been living out an affair with Margaret, his employer's wife. Jack and I eventually found out that this secret relationship had been going on for quite some time. Daisy had already moved out of the house. She had been working as a hairdresser in town when she met Parker. They soon became married. Parker was in the army based at the Barracks in Colchester. He and Daisy moved to Germany, where Parker was to serve his four year required stint. Daisy followed in Dennis and Mildred's footsteps and lived in the barracks with Parker in Germany.

Meanwhile, Mildred's condition was sadly only continuing to go downhill. Dennis never offered to provide her help. Mildred had been dipping into the grocery money for quite some time in order to pay for her beer. This made Dennis more and more angry, and he would yell at her. When he became too fed up with the situation, he would take his army backpack and bicycle to the bus stop, then take a bus into Colchester to buy a week's load of food. There were many times that I felt sorry for Dennis, and this was one of them, seeing him carry a full backpack after a hard day at work. It was soul destroying. Next, seeing the decline of food that Mildred used to cook was sending out more signs of her downward spiral.

I really never knew Dennis as a father or a person because I spent most of my life being afraid of him. Dennis was always hostile towards me. I had lots of ideas and dreams, and not once did Dennis ever try to support me. He was just aggressively negative and non-supportive of anything that I tried to do. I never had a conversation with this "father." What made it even more confusing was that there was another Dennis that I did not know. After my surgery as a child, the doctor recommended that Dennis buy me a dog. Dennis bought me a black collie that I named Blackie. He was my best friend and we spent years of good times together. Sometimes, I even slept with Blackie in his kennel.

There were other times that I saw glimpses of the human side of Dennis. Dennis collected exotic birds and he had an aviary in the backyard where he used to tend to the birds. I once caught Dennis praying and crying in the aviary. So, who was this man? I did not know him and I never would.

We would sit together as a family at the kitchen table at approximately five o'clock each evening. It was confusing for me. I was trying to live a family life, but Dennis was always so irate at my mother and me. I was constantly terrified at the dinner table, not knowing what to expect.

At one point, my mother and Dennis had another dramatic fight, and Dennis ruthlessly threw her out on the street. He gave her fifty dollars cash and that was it. Soon after, Dennis moved Margaret, his mistress, into the house.

My mother, while emotionally, mentally and physically fatigued after so many years, used the money to catch a train to Taunton, in Somerset, where she found refuge with her own mother.

I was overwhelmed by the situation, not only listening to the loud and bitter arguments, but in watching my mother be thrown out of the family home. I stood at the open door, yelling out to her, "Mum, I love you! I'll come and see you!!!"

Without question, the absence of my mother in our home was incredibly difficult and hard on me. It became increasingly toxic to be in the house with Dennis and without my mother. There was a very bad vibe permeating the surroundings. Clearly, Dennis did not want me there and, at the same time, I felt trapped.

Looking back, I was always made to feel that there was something wrong with me and that everything was all my fault. I constantly battled trying to understand this father figure. He never allowed me to be close enough to get to know him. I felt that this life growing up was the way it was supposed to be, as I had nothing to compare it with. I thought this because I was treated as the bad kid and nothing that I did was right. I never really did fit into the family. I assumed that something about myself was really wrong and that I did not truly belong.

When I turned fourteen, my school decided that it would be most beneficial for me to attend the Alec Hunter School in Braintree, which was eight miles from Coggeshall. I took the bus every day, back and forth. That was a good school year for me. I received a lot out of my tenure there and really enjoyed my coursework.

That summer after school was over, I ran away to South End On Sea, which was about thirty-five miles south by the ocean. I worked jobs there at the big amusement park, just as I had done in Great Yarmouth years earlier.

When I came back home after about a month, Dennis said, "What did you come back for?" Dennis, in a fury, set up a meeting in the local court to persuade the judge to legally have me sent away. When I remember that awful day, I often relive the emotions of shock, dejection, and devastation I felt.

The horror and deceit exhibited by Dennis was heartbreaking. Dennis told the judge that I had become too much of a burden to him and the family.

As it turned out, there was no question that the judge had sympathy for me. The judge had to make the best decision for my future. He knew that Dennis had no desire to keep me. Under the circumstances, the judge had no choice but to make arrangements for me to be moved to

Boyle's Court, a children's home and school, located in the town of Brentwood, Essex

After Dennis' declaration, I walked into a room next to the courtroom and shouted, "Why are you doing this to me?" Dennis said, "I love you, but I cannot look after you anymore. This is for your own good. I want you to know that you can never come back." This harsh and cold response set up with the false feeling of love was obviously meant to settle my wrath and resentment, in order for the process to move forward without complications. I quickly said, "No, you don't love me. You set me up."

An important realization regarding this situation is that there were two sides to every coin. I was torn between conflicting sentiments toward Dennis. I naturally disliked and abhorred the way Dennis maltreated me, but on the other hand, I felt a certain sort of allegiance to him as my "Dad," as he was the only father I had ever known. As noted before, in my mind, this was supposed to be "normal." I grew to understand that this is the way it was supposed to be. I wanted to believe, as his son, that Dennis actually cared for me.

Following the distressful confrontation, I was escorted to a van outside where I was met by a driver. The destination was Boyles Court. During the unsettling drive ahead, my thoughts ran wild. Dennis had thrown my mother out. Dennis was throwing me out, too. Who is this man? He was supposed to be my father, yet I realize more than ever that I never ever knew him!"

Later on, I discovered that Dennis gave both Jack and Daisy the inheritance of a trust insurance policy benefit, along with his love, care, and support. I received none.

A New Beginning

Upon arrival at Boyles Court, I was amazed how beautiful the grounds were. A long lane, called Dark Lane, was lined with massive trees that formed a continuous arch over the lane. At end of the lane there was a white house where the manager lived. A long winding driveway led to an enormous mansion in the distance ahead. It appeared to be a castle. After thanking the driver and saying "Goodbye," I was taken to the reception office. I was immediately impressed with a warm welcome. I was given clothes; blue jeans, shirts, and a red, blue, and white checkered flannel jacket. Then I sat down to listen to the strong, but necessary words from the director.

The director said, "What I am going to tell you will be hard, but you are here to stay. It would be unhealthy for you to go back. Most kids who are with us come here to get reestablished so they may eventually go back home. In your case, you are better off to stay here. If you should ever go back home, it would be too unstable for you. You are here so we can help you. We will help you in the best way we can. Also, I need to tell you that your father, Dennis Mower, is not your real father. Under the circumstances, it is recommended that you do not return to him or your mother." In my mind, after that powerful statement regarding Dennis not being my father, I realized that the reason for this news was to protect me after all that I had been through.

I was next taken to my living quarters. It was a shared, large room with bunk beds. After unpacking my bag and getting a feel for my new environment, I was given a tour of the children's home before arriving at the dining room for dinner. During the tour, it was explained to me that this setting was not a prison or a punishment place for me, but rather a home. The fact was made clear that there were two distinct groups of kids. The ones living downstairs, including me, were considered to be the "good guys." The ones living on the upper level were the "bad guys," known as the troubled boys, who had histories of everything from mental illness, criminal minds, and potential endangerment to themselves and others.

In the first few days, I began to gradually process my feelings of "homesickness". I would soon learn what the meaning of "normal" really meant.

In the following weeks, I became comfortable in my new home and I no longer felt useless or worthless. I realized more and more that this was what feeling normal meant and that I never experienced a normal life before. Now, I actually had worth and value. There was no more stress or fear. I began to feel fulfilled and suddenly liberated. The longer that I lived at Boyles Court, the more I embraced the recognition of my good character and goodness.

While living in home for boys, I met another new resident named Calvin. He looked up to me and I could tell he was a good guy. At the same time, Calvin was jealous of me for being so handsome and well behaved. One day, Calvin decided to pick a fight with me. He wanted to put me to the test. Calvin had been bullying me for several days. I easily won by wrestling him to the ground. Calvin never picked a fight with me again. In fact, the two of us become best friends.

There were two other boys that befriended me and there was a strong sense of brotherhood between us. I had a certain aura that surrounded me that other people found attractive, in addition to being drawn to my "pretty" looks, natural shyness, and genuine nature. My new "brothers" liked to look after me. They told me that I was like their little "dolly." They were nice and treated me with kindness. One of the boys used to enjoy styling my hair.

All of the boys at Boyles Court spent time doing hard labor on the grounds; digging trenches and planting trees. I was lucky in that I was never assigned to any of these duties. I was given the special responsibility of retrieving the boys who attempted to run away. It was my job to talk with each one of the boys and help in making them feel better. I was a natural fit for this position and I enjoyed helping others.

An unforgettable experience for me at Boyles Court was in the making. On this significant occasion, I was asked to come to the front office. I was told that, as a special child in a unique spot from the usual, they would not designate jobs for me as they do for the other boys who worked hard labor

I was presented with a very important job and mission. Because I had a track record of successfully bringing back runaway kids and helping them, it was decided to promote me to a calling on the upper level, the high security floor of the home. The boys on that floor were boys who suffered mental disorders and other significant instabilities. As proven, I had a natural way of talking with the boys and was successful in easing their tensions, settling them down, and helping become more expressive and communicative. I was grateful for this promotion, but I also knew that it carried with it possible dangerous risks.

Most of these boys were extremely unstable with severe psychological issues. I undertook this challenging mission with determination and dedication. One of the boys, Frank, was in a very fragile state and was suicidal. I treated visits with him very seriously and carefully. Frank was in a stupor much of the time. He would constantly stare at walls with no reaction and did not communicate. I wanted so badly to break through Frank's apparent barriers and get through to him by using constant reassurance, kindness, and patience. Words did not seem to reach Frank. That said, I engaged Frank with games. Frank could play cards and he would often beat me. There were times when Frank, without explanation, would become violent and would jump out of his chair and lunge towards me. With the help from the staff and my ability to move quickly, physical harm was averted.

Certain boys, in addition to myself, earned a weekly allowance which we received on Fridays. Saturday was our fun day of the week. Usually, about twelve of us piled into the Boyles Court van early in the morning for a lively day spent in the town of Brentwood, about two miles down the road. We called the driver "Cowboy" and it felt as if we were all having a really wild time.

After a week or so, I decided that this weekly ride was much too tame for us, especially in earnest and restless anticipation of getting there. On one of our first journeys, I spontaneously dreaming-up and wrote a theme-like song for us all to sing. I called it, "The Boyles Court Song." Everyone loved it and learned it quickly. It became a joyous ritual for the boys to sing "The Boyles Court Song". We would sing it loudly on every trip to town and back.

Here are the lyrics to my song:

The Boyles Court Song

Eggs and bacon we don't see,

We get sawdust in our tea,

That's why we're slowly fading away!

At six o'clock in the morning,

We hear the cowboy shout,

Get out of bed, get out of bed,

Before you get a clout.

He wraps us in a blanket,

He chucks us in the van,

The van is very bumpy,

We nearly tumble out!

And when we get to Boyles Court,

We hear the children shout,

Mummy, Daddy, take me home,

From this convalescent home.

I've been here a year or two,

Now I want to be with you!

We hear the children shout,

Stay there, you bastards, stay there, you bastards,

We don't want you no more!

Stay there, you bastards,

We don't want you no more,

Stay there, you bastards,

We don't want you no more,

Stay there, you bastards,

We don't want you no more!

When in town, there was much play perpetually awaiting.

We shopped for 45 records, t-shirts, had lunch, and enjoyed going to the movies. It was fun all the way around.

Next, along came Lindsey. I met her in town on one of the early Saturday adventures. There was an automatic attraction. Lindsey worked in the local jewelry store. I used to go to the bus stop and I walked her to work. During Lindsey's lunch break, I was always there to share it with her. We loved every minute of it. When Lindsey ended her work day, I would walk her back to the bus stop.

Sometimes, about twice a month, I was given the privilege of coming back home with Lindsey to spend the night. I savored my stays there. Lindsey's parents were very good to me. They treated me as a future son-in-law. They would always make scrumptious homemade meals, allowing me to help out in the preparation and cooking process. Lindsey's father made homemade beer and he engaged me by showing me his method and giving me taste tests. I delighted in that.

In the following mornings, after a family breakfast, Lindsey used to typically walk me to the bus stop where I would go back to Brentwood and walk back to Boyles Court. It was always a brisk and very happy walk. I enjoyed re-living my memorable visit and feeling very happy.

On one of those valued day and night visitations, I proposed marriage to Lindsey sitting on a bench in town. I was feeling dapper wearing a smart black jacket and she was lovely in her pretty dress. We were mesmerized in happiness, especially when Lindsey said, "Yes!" When we arrived at her parent's home, the news broke into a joyous celebration. Lindsey's parents told us later that, because we were engaged, it was alright for us to sleep in the same bedroom together.

A Turn Around and a Hard Turn

Approximately, a year and a half to two years after I first entered Boyles Court, the time period came when several boy residents qualified for going back home to their families. At this point in time, I had a natural curiosity as to what was going on at my old place and how it might turn out if I went back there. I was taken to the main office to discuss this proposition. I was told that it was not a good decision, and that they were very concerned about my well-being. If I desired to go, they were willing to allow me to do it. Yet, it was made clear that if things did not turn out well, I would always be welcomed to come back to Boyles Court.

The return to the old home was definitely not a good thing. What an eye opening event. Before two days were up, I was on my way back to Boyles Court.

During my quick, and uncomfortable stay, Dennis and Jack were cruel to me. My false father, Dennis, and presumable brother, Jack, were very cold. They almost acted as if I was not even there.

While I was there, I smoked one of Dennis's cigars. Jack told Dennis about this "heinous" event, and that was the kicker for Dennis throwing me out of the house.

In defying revenge, I took off and drove the Mini Cooper that he had bought for fifty dollars all over the corn field near the property. I was crying out in retaliation and enjoying every time the corn hit the windshield. I crashed the car in the cornfield and then I ran off. I walked almost nine miles to the train station. The train would take me back to Brentwood. After arrived, I had a two mile walk back to Boyles Court.

When I arrived back at Boyles Court, I walked down the long driveway and was spotted by several of "Boyles Courters". With enthusiasm, they shouted, "Hey, you're back. Welcome back!" When entering the main office, I was reduced to tears. The counselor said, "Don't feel bad. Just don't ever do it again."

I was more than relieved to be back at Boyles Court. I now truly understood why I had always felt so happy living there. The home was comfortable and I felt revitalized to be back in old my familiar routine.

About three months later, a new boy made his ominous entrance into the home. His name was David G. Another David, but not quite the same as me, David Mower. Not one single bit. David G. proved within a short amount of time that he was not anywhere near an ordinary boy. David G was the hardest, toughest, meanest boy ever to come to Boyles Court.

When the new David met me, it was a wild confrontation. David G. became aware right away of my attributes, as in good looks and engaging personality. It became evident that David G. wanted to be me. He would invariably ask the other boys if he looked like me. Also, he would inquire if the two of us looked like brothers. The response he received was usually the same; "Oh, yeah, yeah, you do!" They conveyed this to David G. because they were afraid of him.

There were several instances that the "bad David" would beat me up. After each confrontation, David G. would threaten me and say, "If you tell on me, I will beat you up again!"

My time living at Boyles Court was about to come to an end in January, not long after my sixteenth birthday in December. There became an availability for two boys to be in foster care at a private home in South End On Sea. The home owners were government social workers who provided "halfway house" opportunities for those in need. They already had two boys in residence and now there would be two more.

Unbelievably, the other boy other than myself that was sent to this new abode was the "bad David!" Needless to say, I was petrified in the knowledge and experience of this knowing how menacing he could be.

I found a job right away working full time at a car factory in South End On Sea. I made black visors that were part of the rear windows of Ford Capris. On Saturdays, all four of us would usually take the train to town to goof around. On one of the train treks, "mean David" engrossed in a despicable act on me. He tortuously yanked me to the outside train door where he forcibly hung me halfway out the open door. David G. proceeded to yank me quickly in and out of the open door. My head and body barely missed the oncoming steel posts. I was unspeakably ravaged by this horrendous and desecrating perversion. David G. was even shaken by it all. I had come so very close to death. This wretched act never happened again.

HELD IN HELL

I longingly ached for the weekend to come around. Usually twice a month I would take the train in South End On Sea to Brentwood, walk to the bus stop, and take the bus to see Lindsey.

On one of those Saturdays, I was eagerly walking while anticipating the joy of being with Lindsey when a police car pulled up next to me in Brentwood. The officer said, "Hi, how are you doing?" I told the officer that I was fine and that I was just going to my girlfriend's home. The officer replied, "Would you mind going to the station with me? I just want to ask you a few questions." I asked "Why?" The officer explained that it was just to ask a few questions and then he would let him go.

When we arrived at the station, they took my fingerprints without saying a word. I was given jail clothes and put into a cell. Startlingly, I pleaded, "What the hell is going on?" I was told that I was going back to South End On Sea and that I was under arrest.

After spending a horrible night in a jail cell, two detectives came in the next day to take me back to South End On Sea and place me in the police station there. On the way in the police vehicle, I kept saying again, "What the heck is going on here?" I was given no answers and it seemed obvious that the detectives were being as "nice" as they could be in order to prepare me for what was to come.

Upon arriving at the station there, I was given different jail clothes and put in a new jail cell. I was to spend two days at this next calamitous venue. Two or three times a day, I was taken upstairs to a room where I was vigorously interrogated by two detectives as to what had happened. There was the "good guy," nice detective, and the "bad guy," mean detective. I was becoming more and more scared and confused, I repeatedly cried out, "Please tell me what this is all about. I have no idea what is going on!"

A form was placed on the table in front of me and I was asked to sign it. I refused to sign anything. There were ongoing intimidating attempts to try to make me sign the form. I never let up in refusing, and never let up in pleading to have an answer about what was the nature of all the harassment. This only brought on the provocation for the "bad guy" detective to hassle me even more. The detective shouted, "Admit it! You know you did it!" My rejection held on tight. The verbal reaction that resulted was a nonstop, battering that relentlessly never seemed to end. The detective said, "If you sign it now, you can go home!" No matter how drained and ravaged I felt, I knew better than to sign that paper.

On the second day of this hellish experience, a doctor was brought in to take DNA scrapings from my body. I was told that they would have all the evidence from the doctor and that when it came back "positive", I would have a lot longer sentence than if I would just sign the document right away, thus, allowing me a lesser sentence. I did not buy it.

No way!

The form was shoved in front of me again and again, with more and more demands to sign it.

Completely exhausted and overwhelmed, I begged again, "What the heck is all this about?" I finally received a response: "You committed the crime. Sign it!"

Angry beyond belief and totally worn down, I looked up at the officers and announced, "Why in the hell are you saying this to me?" I was consequently thrust back into my cell and I became even more terrified.

About two hours later, an officer came to my cell and opened the door. He said, "Get dressed!" After that, he left the cell door open. Hours later, while I was still sitting in this cell, wearing my regular clothes and waiting with the door still wide open, the two detectives came and stated, "Follow us." They escorted me outside. I was told, "You are free to go, and if you ever say anything about what happened here, then we will never leave you alone!"

This three day traumatic experience from hell was very painful for me, not only in the awful memory of dealing with it, but in the anguish of realizing again how wrongfully and dishonestly the whole thing was handled. In essence, I was kidnapped, lied to, and tortured by the police.

When I was released, I felt tormented emotionally, mentally, and physically. I really should have been hospitalized. I wandered around in residual shock and complete depletion before I finally took the long walking trek back to my adoptive home in the suburbs of South End On Sea. In recollection, it had to have been a sheer survival mechanism that kicked into gear. Soon, I discovered that all three of my roommates were victims of this calamity, as well.

The upcoming Saturday, I was more than exuberant to go back to visit Lindsey at her family's place. They were, at the least, ecstatic to see me. It was wonderful to receive their consolation and understanding concerning what I had been through. It felt good for a bit with Lindsey, but then a certain sense of "something different" set in.

On the following Sunday, when I would normally return home after a Saturday night stay with Lindsey, I was afraid to go back. I had paranoia that the police in South End On Sea would come and get me for something else. I asked Lindsey's parents if I could stay over for another night or two. They told me that it was important that I get back to my "kid in care" residence. It was possible that it could mean legal trouble for both parties;, Lindsey's parents and my adoptive parents.

Nonetheless, I was allowed to spend the next two nights there, but it was arranged for me to stay in their shed. Lindsey's family was very much aware of the fragility of my condition and they wanted to help me as much as they could without jeopardizing all involved. They made me aware that I must not stay there any longer than that due to the fact that they could possibly be arrested for kidnapping.

Despite this awkward situation, Lindsey's folks had an unbroken affection for me. They wanted very much for me to stay with their daughter, but apparently Lindsey had other thoughts. She was moving in another direction. Lindsey felt that my circumstances were too unstable. Her parents knew that this entire situation was not my fault. Meanwhile, Lindsey had started dating Mac, the manager of the jewelry store where she worked. Seemingly, Lindsey felt there would be more security with him.

Lindsey and I walked to the bus stop for our final goodbye. It was snowing, and the snowflakes seemed to carry a sting rather than an aura of romance. Even though we held hands, kissed, and stated that we loved each other, we both knew that there was to be a new walk on a new path ahead for both of us.

Lindsey tenderly, yet decisively, expressed to me that she had chosen to leave the relationship. She explained that everything I had been through was just too much to handle. Lindsey told me that she was seeing Mac and that she felt he could take better care of her. We embraced in one last hug and kiss. We never saw each other again.

Nowhere Lies Ahead

When I came back to my adoptive home in South End On Sea, the parents and the boys were very happy to see me, but there were restrictions that followed. Since I had gone over my allotted leave time, I was given a firm curfew. For the next two weeks I was not allowed to go anywhere except to my job.

Soon after that time period, I dreaded coming back home from work during the workday evenings. "Bad David" was always trying to coax me into going along with him and the other boys to town at night to rob the local candy factory. They had successfully done this many times and would bring home their huge load of treasured snow balls. Snow balls are a type of chocolate cake, covered with a pink, spongy, coconut coating on the outside with cream in the middle. I always resisted having any part of it except for one time when I felt uneasy about being threatened. I went along, but I only stayed in the background watching as it all unfolded.

Due to my resistance with the criminal caper, also known as bad David, I knew that I would be bullied again, and very soon. One night at the house, bad David slipped into my room and forcefully placed a pillow on my head, trying to suffocate me. Thankfully, one of the other "good guys" saw this happening and saved me.

I went into deep shock. By the time I had recovered over four days, my foster parents had secured another home for me. This was an emergency adoption and was probably the fastest adoption in the United Kingdom's history.

My new adoptive parents were a married couple, Savanna and Joseph. Savanna was more than happy to take me in because she knew me from work. Savanna was the accountant at the car factory where I worked. She had liked me ever since I first started my job there.

Savanna and Joseph had a small house on the outskirts of South End On Sea not far from the car factory. They were both very nice and friendly with me. Joseph was a long distance truck driver and he would ordinarily be gone on a stretch for several days. From the beginning, Savanna seemed to be flirting with me. I did not say anything, but it became apparent to Savanna hat I had no interest in her. I was involved with Janie, the secretary at the car business. Savanna ultimately understood and started treating me very coldly from a distance.

One day, on my way back walking home from work, a policeman in plain clothes approached me. He asked me some basic questions about my living situation with the couple. Then, he told me to be beware and said, "These people you are living with are not who they seem to be. Be CAREFUL!"

About three weeks later, when the folks were gone, I was preparing dinner in the kitchen and was looking in the drawers to find a utensil.

In one of the drawers, I was stunned to find a gun. I very carefully picked up the gun and took it with me to the woods for about ten minutes. I wanted to test the gun and see how it worked. I fired the gun twice, high out over a tree. It scared me a lot, not only due to the loudness and impact, but to the fear of potential endangerment. I quickly came back home and placed the gun in its original place. At that time in England, it was illegal for anyone to have a gun.

A week later, after this frightful incident, I discovered Savanna crying one night. She was distraught over the fact that Joseph had been arrested for not only drug dealing, but also drug trafficking. This was a much more serious crime and Joseph was in jail.

Amazingly, after two weeks, Joseph got out of his confines and came back home. Almost immediately, Joseph came to me and emphatically said, "If anybody asks you any questions about this, don't say anything!" I went to my room terrified, sat on the bed, and indulged in deep, logical thoughts in my frightened brain. I knew that being a regular drug dealer was one thing, but being heavily involved in the transport of big chunks of drugs from one location to another was a huge dangerous deal.

I realized that I was in an extremely hazardous situation. Due to the unstable volatility of these circumstances, I could easily be killed off by Joseph or any of the people that he was dealing with. I had no choice but to get out of there as soon as I could. I packed my bag, quit my job, and hit the street.

It was winter and that season in England can be miserably cold and brutal. It is not a great season to be without a place to stay. In my bare minimum of clothing and only one coat, I found myself homeless. In anxious need for survival, I resorted to finding refuge by sneaking inside people's unlocked cars in their driveways and huddling in the back seat, trying to sleep. I soon succumbed to miserable frost bite and big warts on my legs.

When daylight came, even on a sunny day, I still felt so very cold. I was constantly shaking. I forced myself to do as much walking and running as I could tolerate in order to increase my circulation. I needed to feel at least a little rebirth of warming.

This horrid ordeal lasted for about a week. Fortunately, I was able to get enough cash out of my last paycheck to make it nutritionally.

With every bit of fortitude that I could muster, I embarked on the train to Bristol. I went to the government office there and requested assistance. Thankfully, they gave me money, food, and accommodations for about ten days while I looked for employment. Unfortunately, as hard as I tried, I could not find a job.

MUM'S THE WAY

Despite these setbacks, I had my mindset on moving forward with a yearning and a plan. I decided at this crossing that it was the ideal and much needed timing for me to go visit my precious mother, Mildred. I had longed to see my mother since Dennis had sent her away from the house in Coggeshall. I had been restricted for a lengthy period; from being in custody of Dennis, to Dennis throwing me into the children's home at the age of fourteen, to being sent to foster homes at sixteen years old, to running away, and ultimately becoming a "homeless child in the wind."

At this volatile point, after getting off the streets, I was finally free. I jumped on the springboard to take the train to Somerset where my mother lived in a one bedroom flat on the top floor at 84 Creech Barrow Road, in Taunton. I stayed with my mother for two months while I worked two jobs. I cooked chicken at a restaurant on Taunton High Street for the first month, and then worked clearing and cleaning tables at a motorway restaurant approximately a mile down the road.

On my days off, I relished my private time. I would venture across the street to a field taking with me my black guitar. I would write my own songs and play them. I felt as if I was singing to the universe.

I called Mildred's mother, Nan. She lived about a thousand feet down the street from mother's home. I especially loved walking with my mother down to visit Nan, which we did quite often. I fancied being at grandmother's house, chatting with her while enjoying a cup of tea.

Nan stated the same thing to me that she had expressed when I was a child. She told me that I was very, very special, and that I did not belong to Dennis. Nan never wanted Mildred to be with Dennis. She wished her daughter had stayed away from Dennis because he was not a good man.

I realized that my mother was a major alcoholic. It was evident that she drank every day. She had the habit of going to see Nan, going shopping, and then drinking. Regardless of what anyone said, Mildred was stubborn and did what she wanted and did not consider the consequences. Occasionally, my mother and I would venture to the nearby pub for relaxation. I was well aware that I should not buy my mother more than one drink nor give her any money for alcohol. Mildred liked drinking half pints of beer.

It became more and more clear that my mother had deep mental problems and refused to get help. Instead, my mother drank to relieve her mental stress. My mind is filled with memories of my mother once being a striking young woman with brunette hair, lovingly preparing food in the kitchen. My mother became an unstable lady with grey and white hair, sitting at the kitchen table with food on herself and rocking back and forth.

Yet, after all of this transformation, and despite my mother being in deep pain, I was astounded over how much of an angelic look she continued to retain, even without bathing or wearing makeup.

I desperately encouraged my mother to bathe. I tried to get her into the bathtub countless times. This became a huge effort and things seemed to be progressing, but before even getting one of her feet into the bath, my mother would scream, shout, and push me away. She used to be so sophisticated and dignified. The sheer thought of someone trying to help her in this state, combined with her obvious mental and drinking problems, was just too much for her to deal with. I was distraught and destroyed over not being able to help my mother. Nan told me over and over that her daughter would simply not get help of any kind. This was deeply painful for both Nan and me.

That same evening, my mother suggested that I get my own place to live. Apparently, she sensed that I was trying to put her in the hospital. Despairingly, I agreed. As I walked to the door to say, "Goodbye," we were both crying uncontrollably. I remember hugging my mother at least ten times before I walked down the front steps. As I descended, I looked back, and our eyes stayed locked. As I slowly went out of sight, I shouted, "I love you, Mum!"

This was the climactic point in my life when I thought my mother had abandoned me, even though I knew that she was very ill. This sorrowful experience brought back memories of the time when the manager at the Boyle;s Court Children's Home strongly advised me not to go back to visit my parents again. In light of this misfortune with my mother, combined with the earlier shocking impression with Dennis, for many years I could not shake the pressing feeling of being abandoned by both of my parents.

As I was walking down the road, I did not really comprehend the dangers of my situation. I was barely an adult with only fifty pounds in my pocket and hitching a lift to London. I believe that the Lord's angels must have been looking after me. I was in an extremely dangerous situation. I remember thinking that my mother was allowing me to do this. I was also aware that she did not understand about the possible consequences that she had placed me in. I remember my mother mentioning that there was something important that she wanted to tell me some day and that she would tell me later when I was older. This comment from my mother, coupled with the intensity of the comments that Nan had already made in regards to me being special, really stirred my curiosity.

THE ROAD OPENS

I hitched a ride to London to search for work. I felt it was going to be a long, homeless week. Along the way, I was invariably being pursued by street drug dealers to buy their heroin. I never succumbed to this as I was too scared and I knew what the consequences could be. Sadly, I experienced seeing other homeless people, both kids and adults, who were in desperate situations. Many of the homeless suffered from mental illness, addiction, or were runaways. It was not uncommon for many of these people to resort to prostitution.

At one point, a wealthy couple from America offered to take me in, but I politely declined. I was just too proud at that time in my life. Almost immediately, I regretted it. Little did I know that there was an avenue forthcoming that would lead to the security of my future and well-being.

I was about to learn about "Job Center". Job Center was a government owned job placement center that provided work opportunities for those looking for jobs. As I was optimistically entering this new possibility, I was more than obliged that in just one day after fulfilling the application requirements, I was given a card for an interview the next day.

My interview was held at one of the hotels owned by the Trust House Forte Group, the company that owns many luxury hotels in London.

In my exuberance, I was immediately hired. I was given a regular room at one of their five star hotels. It was full room and board, plus all meals and hotel entertainment were comped.

After three days of settling into this happy, lovely, and very secure habitat, I ventured into my newfound employment at the hotel. I started out as a porter. My job was to carry guest luggage and other things. Gradually, I was trained in all hotel departments. I quickly became one of the top rated employee in every department during my seven years at the hotel, including being promoted to the hotel's restaurant manager, a prestigious position.

While fulfilled in having this new job position, my two biggest dreams in life were to be a singer and a hotel manager. So, along with the Trust House Forte career, I began taking singing lessons with Arnold Rosendale. One of his clients was Blondie. He told me that I could be the next superstar. On one of the train rides back from Arnold's training, I started crying because I knew that I could not afford to continue on with these lessons. I made the decision to try to earn more money in business, along with pursuing my hotel career. I also heard the words of my real father, Elvis Presley, in my mind about living my life to the fullest and to enjoy singing. This was something my father had told me as a kid on the phone. At that time, I had no idea that Elvis Presley was my real father.

At the age of seventeen, I applied to join the Air Force, but I was rejected on medical grounds. I decided to continue with my hotel and business career.

Right from the start, I made lots of friends who also worked at the prestigious hotel. Out of all the interesting and diverse friendships that I enjoyed, there was something most unique about Alfio. He was an Italian. Alfio was not only intelligent, but very funny and entertaining. He had charisma and a romantic quality about him. He and I developed a fast fellowship.

A group of about eight to ten hotel comrades including myself, spent many great times on our days off, going to wine bars in town. It was a good group. Everybody looked after each other. During these outings, often times someone would ask, "Are you going back to go see your mom?" In my deepest thoughts, going back there was not a good idea. In the past at Boyles Court, I had been told many times not to ever return home. I would answer my friends somberly by saying, "I do not ever intend to go back home again."

One unforgettable evening, I was in Alfio's car with him when he was speeding. A female cop pulled him over. In pulling-off his crazy, creative deliverance, Alfio threw his arms up in the air, speaking only in Italian and bluffing that he could not understand a word that was spoken. Rather than fiddling with the complications of this, the cop let Alfio go, but warned him about being more careful down the road.

Alfio and I cultivated a fun time, about twice a week, going to late night pool bars or halls. This was a whole new scene for me. It was also the first time I saw Alfio in a different light. He was playing the role of a simple hotel kitchen dishwasher to playing the role of a skilled pool player. It was perplexing for me to see this new found friend who seemingly earned much needed income from a simple job to having a whole bunch of money to play with.

It was immediately obvious that Alfio was a very brilliant and champion "player of pool". He was so good that most people would not get a second shot when they played him. Alfio had a strategy, a very sneaky strategy, and it was clever indeed. He would typically start out the game pretending to play badly as the players plopped down ten to twenty pounds. Then, Alfio would challenge his opponents with a five hundred pound gamble. Laughingly, thinking they had it made, the other players met the challenge. Inevitably, Alfio turned on his real power game and won hands down. While gathering his money, he and I would leave rapidly and make our grand escape.

The first time this wild flight occurred, as Alfio was attending me down the fast road to disappearance, I suddenly "caught on" and said, "Oh my gosh, you're a pool hustler!" Alfio's quick response was, "Just keep running!"

I went a few more times to other pool places with Alfio, but I steadily decided that it was best for me to shy away from Alfio. I felt that Alfio was a "wannabe" gangster.

Alfio soon left his job at the hotel. In saying, "Goodbye," Alfio stated that he wanted to stay in touch with me. I strongly felt that remaining in contact with Alfio would be too dangerous. Notwithstanding, I said, "Okay, I love you!"

I did not hear from Alfio for about a year. One day, I was walking down the street and I saw Alfio. He was very pleased to see me again. I told him that I was doing very well at the hotel. Alfio said, "You should come and work for me!" I asked him, "What do you do?" Alfio explained that, with the money he had earned from his pool winnings, he had bought a building which was where he was operating his pool hustling scheme. I immediately turned-down that offer.

In retrospect, no matter what, my time with Alfio was no doubt exciting. Alfio wined, dined, and bought me all kinds of things. The thing that stands out most in my mind was one fact. Through it all, Alfio always protected me. Most importantly, all the wild fun and exhilaration of running down the street with Alfio to avoid getting caught or killed was not worth the risk of death. However, Alfio and I definitely had developed a bond that haunts me to this day.

A NEW PATH AWAITS

Since I was now living in the Five Star employment way, I wanted to be able to enjoy the extra luxuries that others had, such as nice clothes, shopping, fine dining, or just finer living. On the side, I pursued other jobs.

Among these pursuits were my selling things like encyclopedias and vacuums, horse racing/gambling, and a myriad of other things. What turned out to be one of the funniest business things that I tried was selling jewelry on the streets of London. The whole concept was to pretend that the jewelry was stolen in order to create a bigger interest to buy it. However, I used to buy the goods from a wholesale company. The only illegal part was that I never had a street trader's license to sell. When a policeman came along, I used to run off. I once ran into a department store bathroom and dropped the merchandise all over the bathroom floor. Security thought that I had stolen it from inside the store. It took three hours of explaining myself to them before they would let me go. This ended my street trading career.

My next endeavor was to sell whole life insurance through Trident Life. I demonstrated a good track record in selling insurance and my manager wanted me to work full time. I could not do that since I had a new opportunity that had been presented to me. Therefore, I quit insurance sales. When I later ran into my former insurance boss on the street, he smacked me in the face saying, "You could have made a million. You wasted your life!"

The big part time job in the folds was in becoming a private investigator. This suited me well. A partner and I were appointed various assignments, including making calls. We were partnered to portray ourselves as "good guy" and "bad guy." I was proclaimed to be the good guy in our duo.

A particularly unforgettable call occurred one day. The two of us were sent to a business office where the manager of the business was apparently involved in check fraud. Upon arriving at the office, we met the secretary, showed her our identification, and insisted upon seeing the manager. She seemed scared and took us directly to the manager's office. We decided to present our case and interrogate him there. The manager was terrified, so he wrote us a check for the fraud amount.

As we left that office, I turned to my cohort and said, "What's the name of this company?" In hearing the name, I flatly stated, "We have made a terrible mistake. This is not our case!" We promptly went back into the office, gave the check back to the manager, and apologized. We also informed him to be prepared to issue a new check to the other detectives that were truly handling this case. Meanwhile, the man quickly stripped his office of pertinent paperwork and had taken off down the fire escape.

In retrospect, I realize that my partner and I had just received a confession of crime without proper authorization.

With my continued effort to make a fortune, I sold Dolphin showers, Kirby vacuum cleaners, and was a photographic sales representative. I was also a plumber, which lasted for only one day. I carried a full tool box to an older lady's house to fix her washing machine. She had no idea that I did not own a car and had to carry my toolbox two miles to the train station. It was pouring down rain and the toolbox was extremely heavy. Unable to cope with the toolbox for more than a quarter of a mile, I left the box on the side of the road. That ended my plumbing career.

The situation was kind of the same with selling Dolphin showers. On the day of one of my appointments, it was also raining really hard. After calling my customer, he agreed to pick me up at the train station. When we got back to his home, I sat with he and his wife on the couch when the man asked, "So, tell me about the showers!" I replied, "Sir, this is my first day and I have absolutely no idea about these showers, other than this expensive one is the best one in the world for two thousand five hundred pounds." He said, "Sign me up! I'll take one!" After, he drove me back to the train station. I truly considered this as a miracle from God.

One of the last things that I ended up selling were funeral lots. I was trained by a very large religious black. The man drove his car like a maniac with his bible on the dashboard. I was in the passenger seat holding on for dear life and without seat belts. I said, "You're going to kill us!" Without listening, he just sped down the street laughing and shouting, "We're in God's hands, son, we are in God's hands!"

I became so depressed with this morbid job that my sales approach became very direct. I remember interviewing a military man who asked me why he should buy a burial plot from me when he had one available as a vet. I looked at him straight in the eyes and said, "If you want to rot away waiting for them to bury you, then that's fine, but if you die tomorrow, we can bury you the next day!" They both laughed their heads off. Indeed, he did buy a plot from me and I quit the job the next day.

I had the pleasure of meeting and dating several girls during my employment at the hotel. One particular girl, Estelle, played a vital role in my life. I met Estelle at one of the hotel employee parties. I asked her to dance and she accepted. We got along like magic and dated while at the hotel. We fell in love. On our days off, I luxuriated in going to her mother's home in Manchester. Estelle's sister lived in Manchester, too.

There came a point when Estelle's family chose to move back to South Africa. Her mom and father had moved there in their early marriage when he was offered a job in that area.

After Estelle's father died in a car crash, her mother moved back to her original home in Manchester. Two weeks before this decision, Estelle and I had become engaged.

Estelle's mother asked me to venture back with them. After careful consideration, I decided to say, "No." This decision was painful for me. I suddenly did a lot of soul searching and realized that I was still longing to live in America.

The night before the departure from London to Manchester in preparing for Estelle and her family's move, Estelle and I spent a wonderful, yet bittersweet, evening together. The next day, Estelle and I sadly held each other for the last time at the train station. We were both crying, so much that it seemed to never stop. After Estelle left, I went through a really hard time. During a brief period of time, I wished that I had gone with her.

Not long afterwards, I did some deep soul searching and made an important decision. I decided that I was tired of, and not comfortable with, my name as David Mower. After finding a lawyer, I changed my name to David Daniel Boden. I chose this as my last name in honor of a family I had known and respected from London. I desired to carry a new name in order to help erase the childhood pain I still felt from Dennis Mower.

NEW VENTURE, NEW ROMANCE

During my prosperous vocation with the Trust House Forte Group, I always had a strong desire to start my own business. I wanted to start a mortgage brokerage, but I needed a way to sign-up the clients for my mortgage products. I thought it would be a beneficial idea to offer free advice on which mortgage products would best benefit the client under their circumstances. In successfully satisfying the client's needs, I would receive a commission from the company that I referred them to.

This dream came to beautiful fruition during the last year of my position with the hotel; Summer of 1983 to Summer of 1984. I was eagerly looking around for a convenient small office space to conduct this new business. I discovered in a newspaper ad that a person who owned a building on Grays Inn Road was seeking tenants to rent offices. In a subsequent interview with this person, the owner told me, "You cannot afford an office here ,but I will give you some advice. All money is created from nothing, and when you learn how to do that, you will be successful."

He then went on to say that he wanted to help me because he saw potential in me. He was curious to see how far I could go with his endeavor. He told me that he was allowing me to use his office address for mail only, in addition to allowing me to utilize his secretarial services for any incoming phone messages. He also added my company name, "David Boden & Company" to his company's directory.

My business concept proved to be quite successful. I believe this was the world's first mortgage advisory service. It became a model of its kind and was written-up in the London Standard newspaper in 1984 as one of the best innovative business ideas at that time. It is now utilized all over the world.

One evening while I was helping out at the reception desk, a young, gorgeous lady approached the counter to check into the hotel. Her name was Desiree and she was on a two week holiday in London. She had traveled to England from the United States. It did not take long for Desiree and me to strike up an amiable conversation.

A few days later, I took Desiree out for a drink. She lived in Virginia Beach, Virginia, with her family and was a professional model. Desiree had come to London on assignment for a couple of modeling bookings, and also to visit some distant relatives there. This date was the first of many to follow.

No time was lost before my buddies at the hotel jumped on me and said, "Stay away from her! She's a model and way too pretty for you." They were implying that only trouble could lie ahead. There was no possible trouble in my mind. Desiree and I seemed to be developing a relationship together.

In a loving moment, Desiree said the magic words to me, "I love you." I loved her, as well. Then she asked, "What are your plans for the future?" I quickly replied, "Funny you should say that. I have always felt that I needed to be in America and have always had the desire to go!" I told her that I had been saving up with the goal of going within a year. Desiree inquired, "How would you like to go back to Virginia with me?" It certainly incited my mind and heart, as I had never let go of my overwhelmingly, aching feeling to move to America.

Suddenly, I felt that everything was happening at once. I was being immediately and ultimately tested. I had been called upon to report for an important meeting with a large financial company in London. It was apparent that they were impressed with the article in the "London Standard" about my business concept that showed so much promise.

The company offered to buy me out. but desired that I work with them. They were going to give me a salary and 10% of the company. I firmly declined. The company kept after me, saying that this was a one-of-a-kind offer with a big future. I had my mind made up. I ended up selling my unparalleled idea to the company for a cash sum. I had my eyes set on moving to America. It is important to note that this declaration was not based on Desiree's invitation for me to move with her to the United States, but much more on my longtime and ongoing eagerness to go to America.

OCEANS AWAY TO USA

My journey to the United States became a reality in February, 1984. Desiree and I arrived in Washington, DC and then on to Norfolk, Virginia. The whole bracing expedition brought on feelings of being excited and yet scared. A new world lay before me with my new fiancée, but the unknown was a big question mark. I knew all too well what that meant.

Desiree's parents picked us up at the airport. Desiree's mom promptly sensed my shyness and uneasiness. She made an extra point of giving me a huge welcoming hug. After going out for a pleasant dinner, we dropped anchor at Desiree's family home.

Desiree's mom, Victoria, was originally from England. Desiree was born in New Zealand. Her real father, Ben, divorced from Victoria, was from England as well and living in Chicago. Victoria's husband, Leo, Desiree's stepfather, was from Cuba.

They lived in their home with shared children. There was Desiree, Mari, and Parson; offspring of Victoria and Ben. Then, there was also Remi and Meg; kids of Victoria and Leo.

I soon realized that Leo was a tough, macho guy, but he also had a fun loving and playful side. Leo and I got along really well from the beginning. After a while, we discovered we shared common interests, whether it was deer hunting in the mountains, taking the boat out and water skiing, or just spending time on the beach.

When Desiree discovered that she was pregnant, her parents insisted that the two of us get married. On June 29th, 1984, her family hosted a beautiful Victorian-style wedding on Ocean View Beach. It was a wonderful ceremony with family and good friends in attendance. We all enjoyed the live music and natural ambiance.

Desiree and I felt happy, but we both were undergoing a certain uncertainty, as it was not officially our decision. We were urged to quickly make our way to the altar. Unfortunately, there was the lack of a smooth and gradual flow in the relationship. There was also an uncomfortable concern regarding my gender situation. Desiree was originally aware of this unusual circumstance when we met in London.

I lived in Desiree's family home for several months before the baby was born. There was a combination of happy and fun times with Leo. He treated us to family dinners on the town and sporting outings, to disturbing times on the home front. Behind the scenes, Leo was occasionally hitting his wife or verbally abusing her son, Parson.

Leo, on the other hand, never hurt his own kids, Remi and Meg. In fact, it was just the opposite. He stood up for his own blood and he would do anything to defend them when necessary.

Once, someone had stolen Remi's bike. Leo knew exactly who the culprit was. In retaliation, Leo grabbed me and said, "Get into the truck!" We drove four doors down to the "guilty" neighbor's house. As we approached the front door and knocked, Leo told me to stand directly behind him. As soon as the father of that home opened the door, Leo blurted out, "Your son stole my son's bike! Put it in the back of my truck!" With that, the man declared, "It's not your bike anymore. It's my son's bike and it will stay on our property!" Not a second went by before Leo pulled out two guns, one in each hand. He placed them on both sides of the man's head. Leo yelled, "Put the bike in the truck now!" The bike was promptly placed in the truck. As Leo got in the truck to leave, he pronounced, "Don't make me come back!"

I realized that this family that I was living with was an outline of abuse, struggles, love, protection, power, success, failure, and fun. It was lots of stuff. In retrospect, I was never hurt or mishandled at all by Leo. I just had the misfortune of once watching Leo hit Victoria. I always had a continuing sense of being scared in knowing what Leo was capable of doing. I often wondered what might happen next.

It became apparent that even though Leo could be a fun-loving and engaging guy, he definitely had an oppressive element about him. This was most obvious when there was an outward verbal battle between him and either Mari or Desiree. It usually followed a situation when Leo would insult one of them and they would "fight" back in trying to defend themselves.

Despite all of that, there developed a growing personal and professional bond between Leo and me. Leo owned a car repair garage. I helped him at his garage for two years doing multiple tasks before my immigration status was confirmed.

On New Year's Eve, December 31, 1984, our gorgeous baby girl, Allison, was born. It was the most beautiful day of our lives. I stood by Desiree during the whole birthing process and it was an amazing and momentous celebration. We became parents, now a threesome family. I decided to move into a condo less than half a mile from Desiree's parents.

FULL STEAM AHEAD

From the very beginning of being at home with Desiree in Virginia, Leo unquestionably went out of his way to support and encourage me. I had originally applied for my green card, the permanent resident alien card, for proof of residency and which gave me the ability to find employment. This process takes two years to complete. After a year and a half, I was eligible to receive my work permit card. I was able to pursue business opportunities. Up until then, I continued to do various odd jobs for Leo in his car repair business. Once free to pursue employment, I went "hog wild," finding all kinds of vocations. Meanwhile, Leo had a driving fascination for the real estate business. He bought training books to help educate himself in the field and shared them with me. This became an ongoing mutual interest for both of us. While I was working many different positions, Leo was regularly reading and studying all the aspects of real estate.

Early on, before the job activities kicked in, I set off on a "gold rush," seeking good finds to sell at the flea markets with my mother-in-law, Victoria. We literally plunged into trash cans, selecting "goodies" which we took to the market. We actually made some money here and there.

In one incident, Victoria and I thought we had hit a gold mine. We discovered a huge computer with all of its parts in front of a house. While we were in the process of pulling this "baby" out and into the station wagon, the home owner turned his front porch lights on.

Victoria and I quickly hid behind the bins. Standing in his doorway, the home owner could see that something was going on. At this point, I popped out from my hiding spot and said, "Can we have this computer?" The resident replied, "Sure, fine, you can take it!"

Upon taking this "treasure" back home, and in the process of taking it out of the vehicle and placing it in the driveway, all of the metal sides fell off and came crashing down. We left it there and went inside to have tea and biscuits. We discussed how we would put the pieces back together and sell it to a computer dealer the next day.

The next day at the computer dealer's store, the owner informed us that it was an old navy computer and it was worthless. I looked at Victoria and she looked at me. Together, we said, "Let's get out of here!"

The next enterprise adventure was a wild flop. I bought a magazine with business listing opportunities and saw an ad for selling space pets with the lure of making several hundred dollars a day. I ordered a sample for twenty-five dollars. When the box arrived, it felt awfully light as if it was empty when, suddenly, the infamous space pet popped out. It was nothing more than a blue mylar balloon with big eyes and legs dangling down. I thought, well, I will go ahead and give it a try. So, I ordered a few more. Meanwhile, I left one "pet" in the house to float around freely. It floated down the hallway and up the stairs. While I was sleeping in the middle of the night, I was not just jolted, but terrified when the space pet grazed across my head.

As I ventured into trying to make sales with this crazy item, I soon discovered that no one was interested. Nevertheless, I took my space pets to the local flea markets, setting the price at five dollars and ninety-nine cents per pet, which was way too high. The poor pets did not attract anyone. No draw. As I look back at that time in my life, I realize that this was just another lesson that I had learned.

Throughout this period of "professional discovery," I was persistently looking for ideas and possibilities to make an income in order to help support my daughter, Allison. Simultaneously, I continued pursuing other opportunities. Many vocations came about. I sold encyclopedias, vinyl siding, liquid roof repair, and family photo albums door-to-door. I also worked at a Cadillac car dealership. The job ended abruptly after I took a potential client on a test drive which ended in a day-long stay at the beach.

Next, I landed a nice job with ITT Technical Institute in Norfolk as a full time student recruiter. The job lasted a year before I discovered new opportunities.

I found a Bartending School just sitting there wanting to be bought with no money down. The whole place, all equipment included, was just waiting for a new owner. All I had to do was find a teacher, and I did.

For six months, the school went well until one day the bottom fell out. A man walked in, uninvited, sat down and stated that he owned everything. He claimed that the person he had sold the business to owed him money. He showed me the documentation and he also showed me a knife. We got into a verbal fight. The man threatened me and I wanted to retaliate. I realized that I should be cautious. The man said, "You have twenty-four hours to make up your mind. I can make you disappear, and I will." I reviewed the paperwork and realized that the man that "sold" me the school did, in fact, still owe the money for it. I called him, left a message, left the keys on the desk, and I walked out.

Next, employment came calling again for me as a student recruiter. This time it was at the Culinary School of Washington, DC. After a year of fulfilling that designation, I spent three months in Georgetown selling dating memberships. I setup appointments for clients to "show off" their profiles on video for date seekers. This was not an occupation that I liked. Once, an amusing adulation occurred when I asked a female applicant, "What kind of man are you looking for?" She said, "One like you!"

A GOOD SIGN

I proceeded back to Virginia Beach where I landed a career that would finally lucratively give me the steady cash flow that I needed while continuing to build my real estate knowledge.

It all started with an ad that captured my attention about making anywhere from two to five hundred dollars a week selling signs to businesses. It involved all kinds of signs from "open" signs to "hour" signs, to giant signs, and everything in between. Under my own "Boden Sign Company," I launched this endeavor into a fruitful enterprise that carried me through five years of prosperous sign selling from Virginia to Florida.

In the interim, my father-in-law and I were preparing ourselves to propel into the real estate field by absorbing all that we had set out to learn about the program. About two and a half years into my gainful sign business, Leo and I started out by buying twenty houses, some of which we fixed up, and then rented out. This turned out to be a huge headache as far as managing them and not making much money. Plus, the houses were not appreciating. We decided to sell. The next effort was to jointly buy apartment complexes. We brought in Leo's friend, Max, on this collaboration, making for a three way investment. Disappointingly, this venture presented itself with the same worthless issues resulting in not only more headaches, but a migraine.

In realignment, Max went into the insurance business, and Leo went back to running his car repair operation. It was at this junction that I pulled forward the memorable statement that was made to me back in London by the mentor who had taken me under his wing. He had also given me office space for my innovative mortgage advisory service. His impactful words were, "In order to make something, you have to create from nothing!" So, I plunged into trying to figure out how to apply this to real estate.

I bought the books that Donald Trump released. I soon realized that in order to make money in real estate, you cannot rely on the market. A person makes money by buying real estate, not by selling it. Subsequently, I learned how to negotiate real estate very cheaply. I designed a program to do just that, and it worked. I found myself with a program that could potentially make me five to thirty thousand a month, and eventually even be in competition with Donald.

My first attempt wound up buying even bigger, alongside Donald Trump. It was for the Dominion Bank Building in downtown Norfolk, on the water. Trump won the deal. I missed out on a twenty million dollar profit. This would be an eye opening event for me and a definite learning experience. I learned how Donald did it and I knew I could do it, too.

I recall celebrating this real estate victory. Donald came sailing into the harbor on his white yacht. I was overwhelmingly hypnotized by the proceedings and remember saying to a friend, "I could have done it!" I continued to work on this idea with the hope of my making deals come true for myself.

Domestically, Desiree and I were growing apart, which started a year after I had been working with ITT. We became separated in September of 1987. I agreed with Desiree on joint custody of Allison at the time. Allison became a "traveler" having to travel back and forth between Desiree and me. Soon, I moved in with my friend, Max, and his wife, Haley, in Virginia Beach. I held the fort down in taking care of my daughter during her visits. I filed for joint custody of Allison as the divorce filing came into place. A long custody battle ensued. I was ultimately awarded joint custody.

THE SADDEST SORROW

After the divorce, I met Jetta. She owned a house in Keyser, West Virginia. I lived in Virginia Beach. I owned some real estate in Keyser and visited there often. It was during this period that I started to think seriously about my mother again. I always naturally thought about her. Although time kept moving forward, I simply did not have the funds to go see her. All of my money had gone into fighting for joint custody of my daughter, Allison. I eventually ended up saving enough funds to go on this important visit to see my mother. I spoke about this forthcoming plan with Jetta. In accommodating my busy work schedule, I planned an agenda to fly and see my mother in Taunton, Somerset in six weeks.

My mother was heavy on my mind. I missed her tremendously. What I did not realize was that Daisy, my sister, had hired a detective to find me. I had not seen Daisy since I was thirteen years old. I received a telegram from her asking me to call her immediately. I called her frantically and asked, "Is everybody okay? How is my Mum doing?" She said, "Oh, no, no everything is fine. The reason I sent you the telegram is that Mum wants to urgently see you. There's something that she wants to tell you, but she won't tell me what it is!"

I responded, "It's funny you should telegraph me, as I had just made plans to fly and see Mum." Daisy conveyed that there was no rush. She had just gone to see my mother in the day hospital where she stayed sometimes. My mother made it well known to Daisy that she had something to tell me. Upon learning this, I was so happy. I was eager to learn what it was that my mother desired to tell me.

About two weeks before I launched on my highly anticipated trip to be with my mother, I received a call from Daisy. She told me that Mildred, our mother, had just died. I immediately said to Daisy, "You told me that she was fine. What happened?" Daisy replied, "She died of a heart attack due to a prescription medication error. She was found slumped in her chair while watching television." She used to go to the hospital as part of her treatment. When I asked Daisy about how she actually died, she informed me that the doctors marked the death as unknown.

Later on, Daisy told me that my mother had really died of a broken heart because she did not get to see her child. I was sad and distraught, but knowing my mother was looking forward to seeing me made everything seem a little easier to deal with. My mother knew I was on my way to see her before she passed away. I missed my mother so much and whatever she wanted to tell me had just died with her.

ON THE BRINK, TWICE OVER

After living with Max and Haley for two years, I moved in with my friend, Jetta. Not long after I moved, I was able to survive with my signs and real estate businesses. I was driving up and down from Virginia to Georgia, and then to Florida and back. I suddenly developed what turned out to be a major infection. It was affecting both of my lungs and heart. I remember being close to dying prior to the diagnosis of this infection. I was under the physical siege of a "monster" collapse, between pneumonia and sepsis. I learned that this ugly physical "attacker" was actually in the process of strangling my heart. After powerful antibiotics were prescribed, a long six month recovery was necessary. During my illness, I lost a lot of weight.

I noticed that I was coughing a lot during a business drive from Virginia to Florida and back. As my condition worsened, I developed anxiety to get home so I started speeding through Georgia.

I was pulled over by Georgia police and wound up in jail. The jail cell was very small and crowded. They placed me on the top of a bunk bed. I was overwhelmed from this major setback and I felt miserable. I was extremely uncomfortable and I could hardly move within this tight spot, not to mention the fact that there was a radio playing loudly, non-stop, all during the night.

As if that was not enough, the next morning I was taken out of my jail cell and moved to another. There was a big guy in the same cell with me and I quickly realized that he was a "psycho!"

Thankfully, about fifteen minutes later, I was brought out and told to sit down at a wooden table. While sitting there looking out the window, I noticed that there were several inmates in the process of cutting grass. It brought back to mind when I first arrived, when other cell members said to me, "Oh, so, you're another highway ninety-fiver!"

It became apparent that the other highway "victims" had also been taken off the motorway, but because they could not pay their fines, they were forced to do hard labor and stay in jail for at least six months.

As I watched the prisoners outside doing yard work, one of the policemen, chewing his gum like crazy, walked over to the table where I was sitting. He sat down and started mechanically and tediously filling out paperwork in front of me. When the policeman finished his paperwork, he suddenly reached over to a nearby table and pulled out an old fashioned manual credit card machine. He looked at me square in the eye and proclaimed, "That'll be nine hundred and fifty-seven dollars. We take Master Card, Visa or cash, but no checks are accepted." I paid the amount with my debit card.

After I obtained my receipt, the policeman drove me back to the motorway to my car. He said to me, "You can go now." My reaction was, "How do I know that you're not going to stop me again, as I'm still in Georgia?" The officer's quick response was, "If I were you, I'd drive as fast as possible to the state line!"

Several months later, there was s story in the national news warning people who were driving through Georgia that policemen were targeting tourists. It was reported that tourists were routinely being pulled over, arrested, and thrown in jail.

I returned to Virginia Beach for an additional year with Jetta. I continued my work in the sign business, traveling up and down from Virginia to Florida. When Jetta's brother told her that he was moving to Elizabeth City, North Carolina, she and I decided to move there, too. Off we went to Elizabeth City. We rented a trailer in the same trailer park as Jetta's brother, about five trailers away.

Jetta and I really enjoyed every minute of living in the trailer park. It was complete with dirt roads and everything "country." By the end of about a year of being there, while I was still selling signs all over North Carolina, Jetta's brother decided to move back to California. During that process, her brother's dog, a rottweiler named Billy, was left with Jetta and me. The dog was wild and uncontrollable. Jetta and I had no other choice than to find a new home for Billy. With much despair, I learned a few weeks later that Billy had been hit by a car and had died instantly. This was sorrowful and distressing for me. I could not bear to stay in this same environment.

Jetta and I moved down to Fort Meyers, Florida. Prior to the move, it was evident that Jetta was becoming extremely tired and weak. She was also beginning to lose weight. When I came back from an important court date regarding joint custody of Allison in Virginia Beach, I discovered that Jetta was quite ill. She had suddenly lost a lot of weight and had a hard time moving. Our loving and caring dog, Buffy, never left Jetta's side the whole time I was out of town.

After being rushed to the hospital in Fort Meyers, Jetta's diagnosis became clear. She was suffering from colon cancer. A successful surgery followed. Soon after, we moved back to Virginia Beach where we found an apartment. Once a week, for about three months, I religiously drove Jetta to the Bethesda Military Hospital in Bethesda, Maryland. It was a four hour journey each direction for Jetta's chemo treatments.

During the latter part of our living in Virginia, when Jetta was experiencing feelings of exhaustion and weakness, we did not know there was an aggressive cancer growing inside of her. Jetta was experiencing no pain, no symptoms, nor experiencing any discomfort. We were blindsided by her cancer diagnosis.

We finally received good news. Jetta was deemed fully recovered. We were so thankful, especially considering Jetta was once on the verge of dying. On a similar pattern, though, of course, with a different story, it brought back the jolting memories of my prior close call of death with my massive infection. On both notes, the fortunate results brought on a huge wave of gratitude and relief.

FROM PITIFUL TO PLENTIFUL

I relied on the sales of my signs for an income and financial survival. After receiving Jetta's "clean bill of health," it was "on the road again" for us. It seemed I was selling signs everywhere in the state of Florida. It was a life for about a month or so of going from spot to spot, living briefly in motels and barely making ends meet.

We believed Vero Beach, Florida would be a very nice place to live. The fact was, I would not be able to afford it by just selling signs, not to mention the circumstance that this current pattern of existing was just not the way to go. Hence, a new horizon was about to unfold.

Halfway between Destin and Vero Beach, Jetta and I came upon a "For Rent" sign. It turned out to be a kind of trailer park with lots of "sheds." They were actually primitive wooden shacks with tiny porches.

We decided to live in this trailer park. I continued my signs operation, moving around the area and selling to local businesses. Living in these shacks was just about as low as anyone could get. Occasionally, I would visit and talk with my neighbor. He was a construction worker and drove an old truck. It was evident that my neighbor was having trouble getting custody of his children. Early one morning, I woke up to the lights of an ambulance and a police car outside of his shed. I later learned that my neighbor had hung himself.

Approximately a week after losing my neighbor to suicide, I realized it was time to move out of the trailer park. As hard as I tried, Jetta and I had been suffering financially. The rent for the shed had to be paid every week, and our rent was two weeks overdue. Additionally, the reality was that the sheds were unsafe and fragile. During our time living there, the winds of a storm had blown two of the sheds down to the ground. We desperately needed to move

I knew that I had to be successful in order to survive. It was either the streets or success. I had four days left to pay the next week's rent. I was sitting on the shed's little front porch thinking, "I have got to get successful in four days, but I only have twenty-five dollars left to my name."

The dramatic turning point came to me when I remembered the comment that was made to me by the banker in England. He basically taught me that an individual must learn to create something from nothing. I immediately thought, "Oh yeah, I got that covered!" I knew from reading and digesting Donald Trump's books that all I had to do was to get myself out there and do a deal. I always had that real estate knowledge in the back of my mind and it was time to apply it.

The surge of motivation was felt out of desperation. The other powerful motivator was from being concerned about my daughter, Allison. I really wanted to go and get her so she could be with me.

In a burst of enlightenment, I looked at Jetta and said, "I am going to get us a house in Vero Beach!" She looked at me as if I was completely crazy.

I knew I could not make the last two payments of rent and, with four days left on the second week, I decided to talk with the manager. The manager pretended to be the land baron of his kingdom. He acted as a domineering landlord who knew how to keep everything tight and right. In reality, he was nothing more than "the manager of sheds," living in a trailer in the middle of a field filled with lots of shacks.

Regardless, this "shack owner" had developed a "heart on heart" understanding and, eventually, were in agreement. He gave me and Jetta four days to leave, with the understanding that I would make up for the lost two weeks in rent later.

In the first two days, in between selling signs, I cruised around Vero Beach in my car with my focus on looking at different houses all over the area. I knew in my mind that, in order to make this real estate deal happen, the house had to be empty.

In my quest for a house for sale, I discovered a gated community with the gates open. As I drove around the circle of homes, I noticed the home near the cul-de-sac with a "For Sale" sign displayed in the yard. I called the realtor and scheduled an appointment for the next day.

To my wonder, I had found a wooden 2,500 square foot home located in the private tennis court "society". The house was lovely. It had a beautiful open floor plan with cathedral ceilings, two fans on either side of the atrium, sky lights, three bedrooms, two baths, two car garage, and a lawn sprinkler system. Fortunately, the house was empty.

I explored the house while talking with the realtor when I saw a tremendous challenge before me. I knew that I had no money and had no way to make a down payment. I also knew that I could not afford a monthly payment on the mortgage.

Time was crucial and the need to have a place to live was dire. To my delight and astonishment, I learned that the owner had no mortgage on the property. In addition, the owner preferred to have someone living in the home rather than leaving it empty.

Thus, my offer was simple; a five hundred dollar deposit with the contract to be paid by check, and closing on the property in ninety days. The owner would give me a first mortgage on the property with ninety-five percent financing with the rest paid in cash. Then, I added the request to give me immediate occupancy upon acceptance of the contract along with the keys to the house.

The next day, the "bells chimed!" I received a phone call from the realtor saying that the owner had accepted the deal. On that same day, the house keys were secured. Jetta and I moved in within an hour. A major celebration ensued hallowing an amazing creative deal with the remarkable transition from the poor shack life to the environment of the rich.

STRATEGY FOR SUCCESS

It was clear that I needed a quick five hundred dollars before my check to the realtor would clear. Typically, it would take within five to seven days for the earnest money deposit to occur.

Needless to say, I worked very hard at selling signs like never before. In order to play it safe, I begged the bank for an overdraft of four hundred dollars so the check would make it through. I knew I had to make one hundred dollars in a week, which I did. It all worked. Even though Jetta and I were very happy living in an astonishing new home, I was well aware that I had to maintain a high level of success.

Down the street, there was a neighborhood with hundreds of houses. They were worth between $45,000 and $65,000. Typically, each home was a modest 1,000 to 1,200 square feet, three bedroom, two bath, stucco, with white a picket fence. It was the perfect real estate investor's dream area and I knew that my prosperity lay right there. Therefore, I went home and set my mind to designing a plan for each one of these homes to be sold. I also acknowledged that I had to sell those houses fast.

I had created a successful mortgage advisory service in the United Kingdom. I focused on my ability to repair an individual's credit. I had previously proven that many people did not think they could buy a home when they actually could.

In kind, I designed a classified ad that said, "Three bedroom, two bathroom, cute home in a nice, safe neighborhood, $59,900, good, borderline, or no credit is okay." I placed the ad in local newspapers' in the real estate "for sale" section. I knew that I had to have buyers as quickly as possible. I had virtually no money and no houses for sale. I also knew that I was not looking for "fixer-uppers," as I had no funds to fix anything and no houses to fix.

Unlike today, someone could obtain an FHA loan with reasonable credit and the owner of the house did not have to own a home for any period of time before a buyer could buy a home from the seller. Presently, one has to physically own a home for ninety days before they are able to sell it on an FHA loan.

Keep in mind, I did not own any other houses, other than my own, which I still had not closed on. I still needed the money to close on it.

I went to the neighborhood with all the little houses for sale and wrote down every one of them. Then, I had an inventory for houses for sale, even though I did not yet own them.

Phone calls started coming in and people were saying, "We're calling on the house for sale!" My reply was simple, "That's lovely! I am a consultant and an investor. I help people who normally believe that they could not buy a home. I assist them in becoming a home owner and buy a house on a regular mortgage interest rate versus a high interest rate. People end up in foreclosure because they could not afford the high interest rate payments."

Following this, I simply asked a few questions so I could determine whether these folks can buy now, in six months, or in three years. Either way, they will find out if they can buy a home now, or when they will be able to buy a house in the future.

I continued to tell the inquirers, "I work closely with my friend who owns a mortgage company and, together, we will assist you. The consultation is complimentary. You just pay sixty dollars for three different credit reports. Then, after your meeting with me, you will know your particular program. As long as you like the home you are going to buy from me, we should be able to get you into it. Are you interested?"

The buyers would normally reply, "Yes!" I would reply, "Okay, here's what I need you to do. There are two things that are very important. First, drive down to the house that's for sale, and see if you like it on the outside. Here is the address. Secondly, if you do like the house, come to see me and bring sixty dollars. If you are buying with your spouse, that will be one hundred and twenty dollars. Thirdly, if you qualify, I will show you the inside of the house."

I made close to twenty appointments for people to come to my home and fill out applications. Four out of ten people who thought they would not be eligible to buy a home would learn that they could.

Additionally, the potential buyers were so excited over my program that they brought along two or three extra potential buyers with them.

There were literally so many people lined-up from the driveway to the front door of my house waiting to fill out applications that the police showed-up to see what the attraction was.. They found out that houses were being sold.

I truly had to take a risk in the hope that some of the potential buyers would qualify. Before they arrived, I would run out and put contracts on about twenty houses that I had already sent people to see. This method made the homes sell quickly.

The message I told potential buyers was, "If you want to invest in houses, you don't have to go and find a "fixer-upper," because every one of those homes has already been renovated for sale at retail prices with families living in them. Therefore, my deal with each family was at a discounted cash price for the home, a five hundred dollar deposit required, and for the deposit to be held by an escrow agent who would close the deal. The balance would be paid in cash within thirty to forty-five days. I also have the right within that time period to have access to the home and to inspect it."

Because I was an excellent negotiator and was paying cash, I managed to discount houses up to $30,000 each. Also, many times the homes where I could only receive a five thousand dollar discount were actually worth more than what they were being sold for. Thus, along with this discount, I could increase the price of the house to the actual retail price of the house and make $15,000 to $20,000 versus $4,000 to $5,000.

To re-cap, I had twenty contracts to buy twenty properties for cash with $5000.00 in escrow deposits that I did not have. In reality, I had just written checks that needed to clear. I would then control these properties by contract, which would give me the legal right to sell them.

I went back home and the next day I called all of the buyers who qualified under the program to come and sign their contracts. I had so many qualified buyers that I sold all of my homes in one week. Each home was sold under the FHA loan program, meaning that buyers only needed 3.5% down payment. They also paid me a deposit of $3000 on each home, meaning that I now had $60,000 in cash.

I always asked for a higher deposit so that the buyers would not back out, as no one wants to lose a $3000 contract deposit. I only had to pay the escrow company $5000, which left me with $55,000 in cash, and I had not even closed on the houses yet.

This program will not work today because the laws on FHA loans have changed. On the humorous side, I usually would get a phone call from the sellers of the homes asking me if I would bring a big sum of cash for them at closing. I always used to respond, "No, I cannot do that because I'm going to take a nice chunk of money home with me!" We both laughed because the seller thought I was joking.

I strategically cultivated my plan following the Trump method. I unrolled my own knack of buying and selling properties to perfection. It evolved into a track record of genuinely staying ahead of the game in this profession. Inevitably, I brought in steady assets that made my dream come true for supporting my daughter and living a more comfortable life. Happily, I advanced to maneuvering over one thousand properties between Virginia and Florida. This level of success enabled me to go out of my way to buy nice homes for my family, and cars for everyone, including my daughter, stepmom, two friends, and myself.

I went on to consult, buy, and sell over a thousand homes using this strategy. Ironically, mortgage advisers today use a similar credit consulting program that I had designed in the old days back in England in 1984. As a funny side note, I had to be careful about telling investors where I bought homes. I was so good at picking the right homes that investors liked to follow me.

After being so successful with this enterprise, I consulted with other investors who were in trouble with their real estate investments. Simply placing a classified ad looking for investors who were having troubles with their properties, I netted hundreds of thousands of dollars in consulting fees.

Not long after my lucrative success, I stood by my promise to the owner of the shacks where Jetta and I used to live and I delivered the last two rent payments that I owed.

A NEW CHAPTER, A WINNING CASE

I continued selling real estate in Vero Beach for two years. My daughter, Allison, came to visit during the summer. It eventually became time for me to move back to Virginia Beach in order to prepare for the final court date for joint custody of Allison. Soon after, Jetta and I made the decision to split-up. The realization was clear that we were living more of a friendship life than as a true couple. We cared about each other, but we were never in love. Jetta was older than me and was offered a job that made us both feel that she would be secure. She decided to accept her new job and settle down.

I moved into a house in Newport News. In eight months, I was going to face one of the most momentous, life changing events of my life; gaining joint custody of my daughter, Allison.

I made my appearance in court in Virginia Beach and I simply told the truth. I informed the court that I was regularly sending money to support Desiree and Allison.

I also presented the court with happy photographs taken from our recent trip to Disney World. I had included my ex-wife, Desiree, in our trip. We were still able to be a family even though we were divorced. The judge took Allison into a private room where she explained to him that I had always been a loving parent. She also informed the judge that I was a strong provider for our family.

When court was back in session, it became obvious, through Allison's testimony, that she preferred to live with me. It was obvious that Allison wanting to live with me hurt Desiree greatly, but Desiree would still have joint custody of Allison and could see her whenever she liked. I never desired to be in a court battle with Desiree, but I needed to have joint custody of my daughter. I was ecstatic over the fact that I was able to take my daughter home with me. We stayed in Newport News for a short period of time, but I felt that Allison should continue to have a good education. Desiree and I still managed to remain friendly despite our differences.

Fate stepped in and I met Lucinda in Virginia Beach. There was an immediate attraction. Lucinda had two children, Keri and Jennifer. They lived in Salem, Virginia. When we met, Lucinda was visiting her sister in Virginia Beach. I enjoyed spending visits with Lucinda at her sister's home.

Lucinda's daughter, Keri, had been suffering with mental disorders and had tried to commit suicide. She wound up in a mental institution for suicide prevention. I wanted my daughter, Allison, to be in a good school system and I wanted Keri to keep getting the help she needed. I bought a home for all of us that was overlooking the mountains, about a mile from downtown Salem, Virginia.

The house was a gem. It "shone" with a big open floor plan that was dramatic, yet embracing warmth and comfort. The pride and joy was the dining room which had a crystal chandelier and a gorgeous wooden table. The windows had electric candles that automatically turned on in the evening. People liked driving by the home at night just to see the beautiful candles.

Our new combined family got along well, except for the underlying feelings that Allison had about me having "other daughters." The best news was that Allison was able to attend a fine school, Cave Springs High School, which was the answer to my prayer for her. Keri was still very secure at the institution.

The first agenda in my caring mind was to make sure that all the kids were safe and getting a good education and all of the help that they needed. Several months after the move, I made the decision, with Lucinda's one hundred percent approval, to keep Keri out of the institution and bring her home. As time went on, we saw that we could not have made a better decision. Thankfully, I managed to not only help Keri recover, but to help her become a very happy child who did very well in school.

I believe what helped Keri turn herself around was when I looked into her eyes and told her that I loved her and that she had two choices. First, if she continued to try to kill herself, she might succeed. I told her that not having her in our lives would leave a tremendous hole in our hearts and that we would really miss her. Secondly, if she became institutionalized again, she could become so mentally impaired that the hospital may not let me take her home again. I also told Keri that she might be put on prescription drugs which could be damaging, not to mention make her unaware of who she was.

Undoubtedly and happily, this made a shocking impression on Keri. Thankfully, in time, Keri's life took a huge change of course for the better.

FUN TIMES COMING

Moving to Salem and being able to have my daughter, Allison, go to a good school was a tremendous relief for me. Salem is right next to Roanoke, Virginia in a valley overlooking four states. As one comes over the mountain into the valley at night, the Roanoke Star shines ever so brightly over the Blue Ridge Mountains. The city of Salem was clean, the people were friendly, and it proved to be a wonderful place to live and raise a family. Being with Lucinda, Allison, and my two new children, and living in a beautiful new home with a mountain view, life could not have been more wonderful. We were all in a happy, stable home together.

In remembering the good times at my home on Saddle Drive in Salem, it was always a pleasant sensation. Every now and then, when I drove to work, Lucinda and our three kids would follow me in the other car until we reached the mountain pass to leave town. As I drove over the mountain pass, the kids would throw their arms out of the car window, waving them up and down like an airplane. It was an awesome feeling and a great motivator for me to do well for our family.

In more nostalgic moments, every Friday, as joined kin, we went out together as a "family" and chose to either eat at a Japanese restaurant or have macaroni and cheese at another place. Basically, we had a lot of fun times, whether it was shopping in the mall, or visiting friends and family in their homes for barbecues and parties.

Most memorably, about twice a week, we drove up at night to the Roanoke Star. We would all walk over the mountain and pray, making wishes to the Star. These special moments were pure serenity.

I felt that these cherished episodes reflected the first time I had been really happy in a very long time. Naturally, the happiest occasion of my life occurred when Allison was born. That feeling carried forward in the ultimate joy of raising her.

Deep down deep inside, I was still very lost. I had learned to push it aside, as well as dealing with my gender issue. I felt lost in two different ways. First, I had Lucinda and a family that I loved. We were raising Allison and Lucinda's two children, but I didn't have the foundation of what most people have had. I did not know who my real parents were. As a child, even though I thought I knew who my father was, my heart and soul were trying to lead me to who I was, but my brain was confused.

Secondly, there was my gender issue. This was a nice benefit for everybody, except Lucinda. I was a brilliant mother with all of the "mom" instincts, yet still trying to be an excellent father. In dealing with my confusion in my role as a father, even though successful, I had to learn about and embellish on being a man. I had no clue as to how to be a man properly. I knew I was truly a woman inside, but trying to be a man. Being a woman was natural to me. Being a man was not.

In both of these worlds, I had a great understanding of people. I also had a "second seeing eye," had good instincts, and spiritual feelings.

I was very good at "reading" people, analyzing, recognizing, foreseeing, and avoiding dangers. I was fortunately able to always keep the children safe and on track with their schooling. We had a reward system, as many do. When the kids did well in school, we used to post the results on the refrigerator. Allison was good in school, but she had to be pushed a little harder in order to achieve better results.

Allison did not really like the other two children, as she did not want to share her father with them. However, I did feel it was good that she did share me. I felt she could ultimately be more independent in the future within herself while being loving and giving. Allison ended up graduating. I was very proud of her. Everything worked and came into place, and my daughter became a very well-rounded young lady.

In continuation of the good times with the new founded family of Lucinda, our children, and me, I was excited to have Keri and Jennifer in my life. Even though Keri had some problems, as previously divulged, I could see her as a happy, bouncy, intelligent, and talented young lady. Jennifer, on the other hand, was quiet and reserved. She did her duties methodically, including homework, chores, and keeping her room clean and tidy. These factors worried me a little bit, as Jennifer was very often too quiet. However, after getting to know her, I realized that this characteristic was how she gained satisfaction in life. Jennifer still participated in all of the family fun things.

Once Keri became stable and happy, our family could start living a normal life.

When Allison got her driver's license, everybody in the family was so happy for her, and we all went out for dinner to celebrate. The kids fancied their favorite macaroni and cheese at their chosen restaurant.

Our family had many sporting and relaxing times. We had parties at our home, barbecues, pinata events, and many other celebrations together. Mainly, I just enjoyed the thrill and comfort of being part of our family dinners at home under our crystal chandelier. We often visited Lucinda's parents at their house close by, and sometimes also went to visit Lucinda's sister in Virginia Beach.

Once, Keri was driving back home by herself from a holiday when she was hit by a snow storm on top of the Blue Ridge Mountains. She became stuck in the blizzard and needed desperately to be rescued. Her life was in grave danger, as many people can die in storms like this. I immediately set out to rescue her. Luckily, we were on the same road and I was only a short distance from her. When I found her, she was terrified, freezing, and crying. I gave her a big hug and brought her back home.

As parents, we made sure each of the childrens' school life was the center of all of their attention. All of the shows and functions that took place at their schools were marvelous.

One of these special events was when Allison took the stage and played the violin. She had been enjoying her violin lessons at her school for two years. It was indeed a proud moment for all of our family.

Jennifer loved to act. Keri loved to sing. All of the girls' performances were spellbinding. Allison played the violin beautifully, Keri was a rising singing star, and Jennifer was a wonderful actress. At times, the three sisters were in shows together. Of course, Lucinda and I always went to these shows and there was always a standing ovation.

There were also other wonderful times as a family. One of the things we would do to have fun is to wash the cars in the summer time with hoses and get each other wet. Anyone could hear our giddy laughter from miles away. Without question, we were a very happy family at that time.

A BIG SWITCH

In due time, there were hard realities that were seething and building underneath all of the happiness. As stated earlier, Allison resented her two "stepsisters". This was not only because she did not want to share her father, but because Lucinda's two daughters behind the scenes were very conniving. While they were "playing" lovely and wonderful to me, they were mean to Allison behind my back.

In addition to this, Lucinda had been lying to me about many factors involving our relationship. This devastating truth was slowly, but inflexibly playing out in the background of our family unit. In retrospect, it was evident that I had gone out of my way for our combined family. I had bought a beautiful home, purchased cars, furnishings, and clothes. My support, help, and assistance were always available when needed. Of course, I was always reliable in providing an unlimited supply of money. The children had well made it through a fine education. It seemed as if now that Keri and Jennifer were stable and graduating, Lucinda was making other plans.

One day, I was with the kids over at Lucinda's mother's home. While we were having a family barbecue, Lucinda arrived and it became obvious by her behavior that she was having an affair with her boss. Lucinda was the kind of woman who was very manipulative. She had applied this technique on many different men. She actually was appearing quite old due to the fact that she constantly had to lie.

As this stricken discovery began to surface in the last several months of the three year relationship, the foremost tragedy was the fact that Lucinda's children did not want to leave me. In sadness, thinking back, I had a strong feeling about the dysfunction on Lucinda's part. I thought optimistically that I could turn everything around because of the perfect setup with the whole environment; the home, the school, and all theactivities. I asked myself, "Was I an angel myself? I was no angel." In surmising, I was actually lost and was attempting to use this "perfect" family to coverup my pain of being desolate, feeling abandoned, and not knowing who I was.

On the other hand, regarding this situation, and in light of my innate characteristics, being so much like my real father, Elvis; with love, charisma, care, and tenderness, many women wanted to date me. Did I go ahead and date all those women? No. Well, Lucinda thought I did, as she was having multiple affairs.

Nevertheless, I was indeed re-engaging and "playing out" my own scenario on the other side of the curtain. I was doing what I did as a youngster; dressing up as a girl. I used to occasionally go out of town on business trips and dress as a woman. In recollection, I had been dressing up as a girl and having boyfriends as early as I could remember, not to mention my mother used to dress me up for a long time until she was told to stop. I hid the fact that I wanted to be a female for all of my life. In proper perspective, I was not lost as a child. I only felt extremely misplaced. I only became lost, truly lost in 1977 when my father, Elvis, died. At that "intersection" of my life, I took a different turn to avoid the same fate as my father.

I remember being a seventeen year old young man in London dressing up as a girl in a mini skirt. Boys wanted to hang-out and date me. I also had a dynamic charm, as well as a loving and caring personality. I had bright green eyes, bright red lips, a toothy white smile, and velvety soft skin. In general, I was so much like a girl that I had to try really hard to be like a guy.

When I married Desiree, she used to dress me up as a woman because she knew that I liked it. I had always desired for people to know that I really was a girl, both in my heart and in my soul, and had been all of my life. I did not want people to think that I was suddenly dreaming this up later on in life. There simply was not the education or social acceptance back then for me to get help. I tried to be the man that everybody wanted me to be. In essence, I really had no idea how to be a man. When people ask me now, "What was it like to be a man?" I reply, "I don't honestly know."

The family situation with Lucinda and me was distinctively bizarre. Lucinda was having affairs and being deceptive. I was running around being a woman and feeling lost within myself. The children were hating each other behind the scenes. This unhappy dilemma had grown worse in time. The kids were realizing that their parental "rock" was crumbling.

Now, because of all this mess, I knew things would eventually come to an end. For fun and out of curiosity, in still trying to live out my role as a man, I sought out a dating service on the internet. I met Sally. In the meantime, Lucinda was still seeking another boyfriend because she and the former one were not getting along. She ended up finding one. Then, one day, Allison was came back from school to find that Lucinda had moved her new boyfriend into our house. Lucinda had thrown all of our stuff out of the house and on the ground. Kelly and Jennifer were totally distraught and upset, as they loved me very much, and I loved them, too. Undeniably, I was emotionally demolished to see this impact on them.

However, Lucinda had one big problem that she did not think about. I owned the house.

Turning the Tables

I was homeless, sitting in my car with my daughter, Allison. I immediately drove to a nearby apartment complex just outside of Salem in Roanoke, about a half a mile from Cave Springs High School. I rented an apartment for us and bought all new furniture. I registered Allison in Cave Springs High School. We became stable once again in a new location. Allison was actually very content with this situation. She now had me all to herself again.

In the mornings, I would wake up and make Allison breakfast, take her to school, and later bring her home after school. While Allison was at school, I would work on my real estate deals.

I became aware that I had to design a plan for what to do about the house and with Lucinda and the other two children. First of all, I investigated the guy named Seth, who was now living in the house. My conclusion was that he could possibly be dangerous. Lucinda had told me that Seth carried a gun. Seth was a construction worker and did not have the means to support Lucinda and the children, not to mention that he could not pay the mortgage on the house. Why would Seth make the payments anyway since he did not own the house?

In the midst of this impasse, my forthcoming decision was a long and hard one. I confronted a truly challenging resolution that pulled furiously on my heartstrings. I struggled to bring my emotional agenda in alignment with my mental best wisdom. My other two daughters, Keri and Jennifer, lived in that house and I loved them very much. Yet, my own daughter, Allison, who was so relieved to be back with me, totally despised those two girls and was happy to be away from them. This was definitely one of the most soul destroying experiences that I ever had to face in my life.

First of all, I needed to get the rest of my belongings out of the house. I needed to analyze the inside of the home and to also see how the girls were doing. I needed to see how safe the environment was inside of the house. Also, because I still owned the house and technically lived there, I did not need a court order.

Without a doubt, this situation had all the earmarks of being a conceivable hazard. I was raised and trained by the Army Cadets and was brought up in a family of trained and decorated marines who taught me how to survive. Thus, I made the big plan to go into the house and leave with my mission accomplished.

I got into the house, dissected every room, retrieved a few of my things, and left. As I was leaving, one of Lucinda's friends, Charlotte, who was inside the house, was entering the garage door to go out of the house as I was leaving the garage to go out into the street. I quickly ran to my car while Charlotte screamed, "David's here!" As they chased me down the street with weapons, I jumped into the car and spun off. Lucinda called the police. When the policemen later arrived at my apartment door, in the understanding that it was my house where this incident occurred, they simply told me not to do it again. Fortunately, I did get the information that I was seeking.

Conclusively, as time rolled along during an eight month period, it became crystal clear that Lucinda's boyfriend, Seth, did not actually want to live there at all. He certainly did not want to make the house payments. He could not afford them anyway. Most significantly, Seth had lied to Lucinda and told her that he had more money than he did. His inner goal was to move her and the girls out of that house and into his own home in Winchester, Virginia, which is known as "Patsy Cline territory."

I knew that I needed to give Lucinda a nudge. There was no way that I would ever be making payments for another person living in my house with my children. In dealing with all of this, my well devised plan was to wait for the foreclosure, which takes nine months, and then go back and buy the house back from the bank. Foreclosure would have evicted her.

Understandably, I abhorred doing this to Keri and Jennifer, but I had no choice. Lucinda, in her furious outrage over this plan, sued me. I hired the best attorney in town and won on every account. I also got the house back. Because his daughter did not want to live there, and I did not have my other two girls with him, it was way too much of an emotional distress to even think of living in that house again. The original magic of the home was gone. Harsh reality was setting in. The home was now just a house.

I still hung onto the hope that Lucinda, Keri, and Jennifer would ultimately move back in with me. Keri and Jennifer were so fond of me that they even wanted to change their last name to mine. Even though I knew that would not sit well at all with my daughter, Allison, I fantasized that maybe the three girls would get along somehow.

Lucinda talked the kids into moving with her into the home of her boyfriend, Seth, who lived in Winchester. I was so distraught over losing Keri and Jennifer that I just let the home go back to the bank. Lucinda let me see the girls one more time before they moved. Keri was very angry with me and, when I left them, it really made me feel as if I had screwed things up. I simply could not allow a man to live in my house with my newly found daughters.

The move of Lucinda and the girls to Seth's place in Winchester lasted for about six months. Seth threw them out and Lucinda and the kids ended up living with her sister in Virginia Beach. I simply could not put up with Lucinda's lies. Through the grapevine, I found out that Seth could not get over what Lucinda did to me. This showed me that he was somewhat of a decent man. I still wanted so badly to get Keri and Jennifer back, but Allison put her foot down. Allison stated that she never wanted to see either of them again. Allison exclaimed, "Can't you see what they all did to you?" I said, "Okay, I will do what you want." Of course, I adored Allison with all of my heart and soul. However, I also held a special place in my heart for Keri and Jennifer.

One of my best friends in Virginia Beach passed along the information to me that Keri was doing karaoke singing. I sent a message through my friend to Keri that Keri had a super star voice and said that she should go for her dreams of being a real singer. I had hopes of one day turning on the "telly" to see my daughter, Keri singing. I will always have a dear spot in my heart for Keri and Jennifer.

OLD STOMPING GROUNDS

After this overwrought saga, it was now all about digging into the new life, space, and time for Allison and me in our apartment in Roanoke. As Allison attended high school, with one year before graduation, I spent my days taking her back and forth to school, working in real estate, and doing the usual family things. We would go out for dinner, visit friends, play board games, chess, checkers, and cards. There was another company as well as my real estate business that I had organized when I was living in Salem. I named it "T-A-Can-Co International Corporation." It was an investigative and debt collection company.

I was also developing a new relationship with Sally, whom I had met online. She lived in Melton Mowbray of Leicestershire, England. At the time, she was a human resource manager at a hotel. She had a daughter and a son from a previous marriage. She also wrote articles on the subject of human resources and business courses. She was highly recognized for her innovative talent in designing business programs to help women get back on their feet.

I arranged to go to England and meet Sally when Allison was basically out of school in the summer, except for taking a few summer courses. I felt good about the time I spent with Allison before my upcoming, two week jaunt to England. I felt confident that Allison would be safe. I trusted her judgment regarding our friends in the Roanoke Valley.

I flew to London and took a train to Colchester to visit with Sally who drove from Melton Mowbray to meet me. I had three reasons for this location, which was a neutral and mutual spot to meet. First, I desired to visit my older sister, Daisy, who lived in Colchester. Secondly, I felt like going back to Coggeshall where I had spent my childhood and play on the swings in the park. Lastly, I intended to see the man I had thought to be my father, Dennis Mower.

I soon found out that I was not allowed to go to the house. I had to put a plan together for all of that through Daisy. There was nothing official or anything. It was just a matter of satisfying Daisy's wishes. Also, there was the warped matter that Dennis's wife loathed me because I loved my Mother.

The immensely strange thing about all of this was that I was, yet again, following Daisy's rules. She had kept me from seeing Dennis each time I had tried to come back and visit. I was only able to see Dennis one time in town for no more than one minute. In that meeting, I felt like I was looking at a stranger whom I had never known. This disturbed me greatly. Why was I looking at a man who was a stranger in my eyes. I had no feelings or connections with Dennis whatsoever?

The biggest quandary was that Daisy and Jack had always kept Dennis to themselves. I still could not figure out why I was kept out of the family. Why was everyone more cold and aloof towards me? It was as if they knew something that I did not know. I had always tried so hard to give my all and to be loving and caring to this family. It just seemed as if nothing ever worked. It perpetually seemed as if they all lived on another planet, keeping me at bay. I knew that I was not a bad person, even though Dennis, Jack, and Daisy frequently told me that I was. They made me feel isolated numerous times. Ironically, everyone outside of the family welcomed my presence with open arms. I was told that I was a lovely, kind, and loving person. Way down deep in my soul, I had a sense that Dennis was really not my father.

There were so many times that I tried to connect with them. An analogy to my feelings was that I felt as if I was "calling an office and the boss was out of town." I had almost no connection, even though I tried so hard to create one but was repeatedly left baffled and worn out from trying. Undoubtedly, I made a huge undertaking to engage in a family that did not seem like my own family at all.

Quite critically, I also had no idea about what it was like to have a loving family. I kept hearing other families say that they loved their family members with great warmth and intensity, and could not live without each other. I could not comprehend that, as I did not know what it meant. In fact, I had never really concentrated on my thoughts about it or mentioned outwardly that I loved my family. I was subconsciously pushing in my heart to love them all, but it was an exhausting effort. It was also a one way street.

Daisy, presumably being the protector of the whole family, spent most of her time giving me excuses for why I could not see everyone, and why it was not right. Any attention that I did receive from her directly was just a "pacifier" to always keep me out of the circumference.

I looked hard in the face of my existence. The sheer truth was that there was no reason in the world that the family should have made me feel disowned. I had always been a very loving, caring, and supportive human being. Dennis, Daisy, and Jack were always very cold, distant, and uncaring. Daisy had a way of putting on a "plastic" show of care which anyone could see was clearly fake.

NOSTALGIA AND MEMORIES IN MAKING

Before Sally and I met in Colchester, I spent two nights with my former sister, Daisy. Her home was in the same town, known as the main army barracks to Germany, Iraq, and other military destinations. I was not only settling-in after jet lag, but refreshing in the anticipation of meeting Sally. While there, I had the distinct, emotional event of going to my mother Mildred's grave. I brought various flowers and placied them on her special spot. It was quite a moving time at the grave site as I spoke to her about the past, the present, and the future.

Next, in priority after visiting my mother's place of rest, was my revisiting the park in Coggeshall where I loved swinging on the swings as a kid. I walked to the park, reminiscing about the past and retracing my steps. This was the place where I used to swing, laugh, and sing. I found ladies swinging on the same swings and laughing with each other just like the old days. To my surprise and astonishment, these ladies were the same girls that I experienced this with at this same spot growing up. Also, there were parents of the other kids there that I knew. I asked them, "Do you know who I am?" The response was, "What is your last name?" I answered, "My adoptive name was Boden, but my name growing up was Mower. My father's name was Dennis from Tey Road."

They immediately pointed to an older woman who looked like my mother. I had never seen her before. They referred to the fact that she was a Mower. I walked up to her and asked, "So, you are a Mower?" She said, "Yes!" I replied, "I'm Dennis's child." She emphatically looked at me with a secretive, yet direct look and stated "You were never a Mower!" I kept a brave face, held onto my dignity, and slowly walked back along the park trail to the road, while crying. I was thinking in my muddled mind all over again about how much I felt that I did not exist. I thought the ladies were probably wondering why I left so abruptly, but I wanted to cry. I did not let them see that.

In wiping my eyes, while in the process of cheering myself up, I ventured to Norman's Sweet Shop. It was not only still there, but it still had the same owner and the same good old sweets.

The next stop was to meet Sally. There she was, sitting in the George Hotel lobby in Colchester. I walked up to introduce himself, gave her a quick hug, and then told her that I would be right back after I went to the restroom. Once there, I looked in the mirror and said, "I don't like her." I thought to myself, "How do I get out of this? Do I run out the back or front door, or what?" I immediately felt guilty because she had come a long way, and I had already told her that I loved her. I could not just run away. Plus, the realization was that I had previously left Daisy's place and was planning on moving in with Sally at her home which was two and a half hours away in Melton Mowbray.

The truth was that I did not want to disappoint her. I asked myself, "How bad could it be?" She was a very pretty lady and I knew that I needed to get to know her. I pulled myself together and went back to her vantage point in the hotel lobby. I said, "It's very nice to see you in person." Next, we started engaging in conversation. I began to really like her. She had a genuine, personable nature and was filled with beauty, inside and out. After about two and a half hours of conversation, we decided that we liked each other. We kissed and held hands. Next, Sally said, "Let's go home."

During the car ride to Melton Mowbray, there was a mutual feeling of coziness and happiness in anticipation of what the future would bring. Upon arriving, I enjoyed Sally taking me on a nice tour of her three bedroom, red brick house in an upper class neighborhood just outside of town. Sally introduced me to her son, Pierce, in his early twenties, who lived there part time when visiting from his flat in town. I was pleased to also meet her daughter, Abby, who was nineteen and getting ready to go to the university.

The two week time with Sally became a favorable and pleasurable routine. We enjoyed dinners at home, as well as at restaurants, along with shopping, and entertainment. Sally had formerly been in a physically and mentally abusive relationship with her then ex-husband, Sergio. Sally felt calm and was comforted to have me there with her. I seemed to provide her with a sense of contentment and security.

One time during my stay, Sergio arrived unexpectedly. I let him in and it was evident that he wanted to meet me. I shook his hand and made it clear that Sally was now my lady and no longer his. Sergio soon left with his "tail between his legs." My immediate reaction was that I had taken care of business. I confirmed Sally's acknowledgment that Sergio was a control freak.

On another day, I had the chance to meet Sally's mother. We used to go to her flat or meet her in town. She was a simple lady and set in her own ways. Her lifestyle had always been very simple. She enjoyed going to the store, coming back home, watching television, and taking naps. It became obvious that Sally had managed to get herself into a better life.

Leicestershire is known for its famous pork pies and Leicestershire cheese. The area was quite old and sophisticated. Dining out was not just a delectable experience. but full of history and a high caliber lifestyle. One of the wonderful things that Sally and I loved to do was to go the general and antique auctions. While there, we would partake in the auction action while developing friendships with fellow bidders. We had a marvelous time buying all sorts of antiques and treasures of a lifetime, which usually turned out to be a bunch of rubbish.

In the general auctions in particular, we used to get carried away and come home with boxes of miscellaneous junk that we would eventually put back in the auction. On the other hand, at the antique auctions, we would buy more treasured items, such as antique clocks, framed paintings, and bits of things retrieved off of ships. In fact, my presence became so popular that I was invited to appear on the British version of the Antique Road Show. I "performed" as being an active bidder.

ISSUES RESURFACE

On one afternoon, when I was walking home from town, I started to feel dizzy and lost. In addition, I wondered about possible mistakes that were made in my childhood surgery.

As a boy, my genitals were "corrected" to make me more of a boy. In doing so, the ensuing testosterone should have run through my body, helping me be a more normal man and to be able to have children. The fact was that I was essentially a girl living in a boy's body. If there had been the technology that we have today, they could have determined that I was better off being the "girl" inside my body that I am. With the proper corrections, the new "she" could have lived a very normal life without all of the confusion and subsequent physical and emotional agony.

It had become quite clear in my experience that gender is not solely based on genitals. It is mainly based on one's chemical makeup, as well as the brain. Additionally, I felt that it was also based on the important element of the soul. When I later changed to be the gender that I was supposed to be, the science was finally available. The doctors determined that I indeed had a female mind and composition, and that I would live a far more normal life as a woman than in trying to stay as a man, constantly battling how to figure out how to be a man with a female mind.

It became extremely evident that my body was struggling to fight off the testosterone that was gradually building up inside me following my boyish surgery as a child. The physical chemistry in my body was in a fighting turmoil. So, now, all these years later, feeling confused and misplaced, the testosterone was reaching high levels in my female makeup and it was making me become increasingly dizzy and nervous. I had for so long been dealing with a growing insurgence of nervousness and feeling easily agitated because these male levels of testosterone were not only not normal in my body, but significantly invasive to it. The testosterone that was originally intended to make me more of a boy was starting to make me very ill.

Of course, I did not know all of this at the time, and I had become accustomed to living with this uncomfortable life. I just assumed that I had some kind of medical issue that needed to be addressed. I just pushed myself onward, as if there was not much going on. Yet, the prevailing and outward unknown reality remained that I was a very lost person who also had a major gender issue, and I was despairingly trying to live a normal life as a man.

LEAPING OVER HURDLES

Even with all of my physical discomfort, anxiety, and extreme nervousness, I pushed myself to focus on the plan of taking Sally to America, and to meet my daughter, Allison. Upon arrival at the apartment in Roanoke, it was a warm welcome and an immediate feeling of acceptance and friendship. After several days of being back at home in Virginia and spending quality family time together, I took Sally to Virginia Beach to meet my friend, Grant. We partied for a few days and had lots of fun. In returning back to Roanoke, we spent more family time before Sally went back to the United Kingdom with the understanding that I would venture back to see her again as soon as possible.

I continued my ongoing real estate business while intensely working with Allison as she prepared for her high school graduation. After quite a lot of work and dedication, mixed with challenging components of frustration, and impatience, Allison got the much awaited news that she had passed and was going to graduate. I did not realize how much stress she was enduring while she tenaciously, yet, reluctantly faced the aim for her eventual diploma.

It became apparent that I was putting her through too much pressure. Allison, in some sense, was searching for relief and a "way out." That is when she met her boyfriend, Scott. Allison had no reservations in making Scott aware of this. Scott seemingly earned the title of the love of her life. She clung to him as he listened to her avidly and gave her the avenue of attention. As an emotional result, however, she and I both felt this as a tear in the fabric of our relationship.

While I was diligently organizing and pulling together details for her graduation, Allison would occasionally run away to be with Scott at his house. In only a few weeks, I discovered that Scott, behind the curtains, had a past of aggression. He also had an excessive possessive behavior. In anguish, I held onto this tormented, temporary decision to hold things tight for a while. I was right in the middle of thoughtful ideas in planning for Allison's graduation, including a very special surprise for her. I definitely did not want anything to get in the way or throw things off track.

One evening, Scott brought Allison and two of his friends over to the apartment to pick up a few things of hers. The friends acted like guards and they looked at me as though they had the intention to harm me. In harsh consideration of Allison's rebelling and Scott's devious and jealous mind, I recognized that this had the potential of being a very dangerous situation. I was immediately riddled with emotional torture. This incident brought two major facts to the surface.

First, I had so heartily been focused on Allison's sense of well-being and excitement over her soon to be becoming a "grad," as well as my consuming thrill in putting together the best celebration ever for my daughter.

Secondly, I was dealing with major concerns about Allison's personal life. I naturally was deeply concerned and wary about Scott and his problematic personality and dysfunctional personal history.

I knew that I had no choice but to allow my daughter to make her own decisions. I asked Allison to come back to the apartment and have a chat in regards to her imminent graduation proceedings.

This was my opportunity to tell Allison how much I trusted her judgment, decisions, and in her becoming a responsible adult. I felt strongly that she was feeling pushed into finishing school at the same time that she was feeling very much in love. The confusion in her mind at the time was twofold. She thought she knew what she wanted; to graduate, and to be with her true love. Although I did not make this an agenda with Allison, I felt that her boyfriend had very manipulative ways.

In still struggling with the fact that I did not feel well with increasing feelings of dizziness and nervousness, I continued with the graduation plans. On the big day, I treated Allison with new clothes, a full salon beauty treatment, and lunch at her favorite restaurant. The ceremony was filled with hundreds of graduates on a big stage, each one happily receiving their diplomas. I felt really proud to see my daughter in line, walking up to get her diploma. Allison looked at me when receiving her diploma. In her big gleaming smile, she was back with me as a close father and daughter team.

After the graduation, I had arranged for a private limousine to take her to her special graduation party at a five star Roanoke hotel, for which I had pre-invited all of her family and friends, including her mother and grandmother and my best friend, Grant. In the limo, Allison was presented with two dozen red roses. Scott had deviously tagged along in the limo and attended the party.

After the hotel party, the limo took Allison, with Scott again "crashing" along, to her favorite Japanese restaurant for dinner. About twenty members of close family joined us at the restaurant. During dinner, I suddenly felt ill. I was having even more hyper feelings and dizzy spells. I was beginning to really become worried. In the back of my mind, I was thinking that maybe this was what it was all about": getting my daughter through her graduation and then letting myself go to die. Obviously, the angels in Heaven had a different plan for me.

In leaving there, the limo proceeded to take Allison, with Scott, on a stroll to the Roanoke Star. To her tremendous surprise, they were met by the local press and paparazzi. It turned out that they had mistaken my daughter for Cameron Diaz. This crazy phenomenon wound up being a fun twist for Allison. In due time, after taking in the joy of the "Star," the limo brought them back to the apartment.

On her arrival, she jumped out of the limo in utter surprise to discover a brand new red, Toyota Celica GT waiting for her in the driveway. Allison was ecstatic while she was looking at me standing next to the car. I proclaimed, "Congratulations to you, my sweet daughter, on your graduation. Here's your new car, your personalized license plates, and your free and clear title to the car." Without hesitation, Allison joyously ran over and leaped into my arms.

MAJOR DECISION

The very next morning, I noticed that something was different. I said to myself, "There is no more school. There is no more anything." Allison was now spending time with Scott most of the time. My original goal was to try to get Allison to go to college, but at this juncture, I was feeling weak, ill, down, and depressed. As the week progressed, I realized that my job, thus far, had been accomplished.

I had come to a crucial point in my life. Allison was becoming a young adult, trying to make decisions for her own life. She was eighteen years old and I could not force her to do anything she did not want to do. Additionally, I was naturally feeling lonely and depressed, being suddenly all alone in the apartment. All of the busy activities of addressing Allison's needs of daily life was over. Education and preparations for graduation had ended. I was going through "post-graduation depression." My next job was to support Allison in a new way and to try and guide her. In my eyes, there are two types of children; the ones that want to stay home after graduation, and the ones who are very independent. Allison was very independent.

In the past, even though I was feeling lost within myself, I could hide all of that by raising Allison. My job was to support her and getting out there and making money. I had truly been more of a mother to her. I had been strong in "fathering" Allison, but not firm and mighty enough. There is a difference in the way that a mother and a father raise a child.

After a two weeks went by, I became more and more lonely and the apartment seemed very empty. I was not feeling very well and Sally was lurking in the background. In recognition of these thoughts and feelings, I also took into consideration that my daughter needed some time to work things out with Scott. As a parent, I comprehended that one of the worst things one can do is to try to rip one's child away from the person that he or she loves. I fully understood that both of them had to work it out for themselves. I knew that there was nothing that I could really do. As a parent, I had no choice but to let it run its course. As excruciatingly difficult as this was for me, I came to the realization that this was the best decision.

I asked Allison to come and see me at the apartment. She showed up at the designated time with not only Scott, but with four of his friends. It became apparent that, in light of Allison feeling former pressure from me during the process of attaining her graduation, she had well informed Scott about this. Thus, Scott enlisted these buddies to come along as a "back-up" in case there might be any emotional or physical episodes. During the visit, there was an "air" of impending aggression from Scott's friends. It became evident that the group was looking for possible trouble. To my relief, there was none.

I did not feel at all free from the whole situation. I could see in their eyes that they wanted to come and get me at some future date, maybe when Allison was not around. Even though I had vehemently expressed to Allison that Scott had the capabilities of being a potential violator of me in order to keep her under his control. Sadly, Allison did not have the capacity or desired inclination to see the dangers that she had just placed me in with Scott. She was blindly in love. Allison was becoming increasingly brainwashed by Scott and totally unaware of the whole situation surrounding her. Since I had tremendously spoiled her and treated her like a princess growing up, she had become a spoiled brat, out of control, and she was not taking responsibility for her own actions.

It became more and more obvious that Allison was allowing Scott to immensely run and command her entire life. I made it clear to Allison that I could see that he was a very dangerous person and could easily put her family in a very precarious danger zone. So, in my decision to diffuse the situation, I told her and Scott that I had chosen to go to England for a couple of weeks so that they could work out their relationship. In this major decision, I felt strongly that this was the best resolution in order to give the two of them the opportunity to "see the light." I did this for other reasons, too. Because I was not only feeling down and depressed, but also in fear of being harmed, I was off to England to see Sally. I gave Allison a huge hug and told her to call me every day.

Before I left, I asked a few friends in the neighborhood to watch after Allison. I asked them to keep an eye on her and be aware of any changes or problematic issues that might occur. Another reason why I felt that it was appropriate at this time to go back to England was because I was experiencing these increasing feelings of dizziness and instability. I did not want it to be a burden on Allison. In my mind at the time, I wanted to maintain my strength by moving back to my homeland for a much needed break in my life moving onward.

A BIG JOLT

In England, my life became a little bit restored again. I was with Sally in her home, enjoying my life, and helping her support her daughter, Anna, as Anna approached college. Sally and I quickly made friends with folks whom we developed a pattern of spending time with. We used to readily eat out at fine restaurants, local pubs, and hotels, as well as attend local antique auctions.

I was quite happy and I regularly stayed in contact with Allison, who always confirmed that everything was "fine." Because of my unusual and frightful upbringing, I had always learned to stay in "survival mode." I was always holding on, pushing forward, and staying strong, regardless of how I felt medically. Yet, one day, while walking through the town of Oakham in the county of Rutland, I felt more dizzy than I had ever felt before. I was used to feeling dizzy many times, and I had always turned to my self-mechanism of dealing with it, rising above it as best I could. This time was very different and I noticed that it was steadily becoming a lot worse. In an effort to relieve the symptoms, I took natural calming pills from the local health food store. I also engaged in a swimming routine at a local country club, as well as a normal regimen in running, biking, and "getting drunk." This whole combination seemed to alleviate my symptoms.

My two week stay was almost over and it was time to move back to the Unites States. I was eagerly anticipating to see how my daughter,

Allison, was getting along, and also how her relationship with Scott was doing. I was definitely very excited about being with Allison again. During my brief stay in England, I was silently and constantly worried about her and what she was going through.

When I arrived at the apartment, I was surprised to see Allison waiting outside with tears in her eyes. As I approached her, she began apologizing to me. She said, "Sorry, Dad! Sorry, Dad!" She walked me around the corner to her car and I saw that the vehicle had been totaled. The destruction of the car was obvious. At that moment, I did not care about the car at all. My immediate reaction was relief and thankfulness; Allison was alright. I was not angry. I was basically totally terrified that she could possibly have been killed. I saw that all the tires had been blown out. In trying to make her feel better, my comment to her was, "I've just got one question. How did you manage to blow out all of the tires at the same time?" She looked at me and said, "I don't know, Dad!" The answer to that question is still a mystery to this day.

Allison started crying again, and I said, "It's alright. I'm just glad you're alive, and I don't care about the car!" That is when she pointed to my car in the distance. We walked over to it, and the whole front of the car was wrecked. It became evident she was responsible for the accident and had damaged people's property. I still looked at her and said again, "I am so grateful that you are alive!"

The total damage was approximately $120,000, including settlement payoffs for potential lawsuits.

PROPELLED TO CHANGE

I spent several days praying to God, thanking Him for sparing Allison's life. I was incredibly grateful to the car companies who were now building safer cars. I wanted to help Allison understand how very dangerous the whole situation was and how very lucky we were that she was able to payout the difference after what the insurance covered, not to mention the ultimate settlement costs.

I fixed my car and I made it clear that Allison could no longer drive my care. I gave her the former license plate from her car as a reminder that she was an extremely fortunate young lady. I was in post dramatic trauma by the whole situation, but I also knew it could have been so much worse. I could not help but keep drumming this into Allison's mind over and over. I later realized this was "overkill." I soon regretted that I was pushing the punishment for much too long, but I felt at the time that I had no other option. I was afraid for my daughter and concerned about her safety. A classmate and friend of Allison's was involved in a car crash and was killed about six months earlier. It was a huge reminder of how things could have turned out differently for Allison.

It later became apparent that Allison was secretly leaving at night through her bedroom window to be with Scott. I was so worried about this that I requested she come back to the apartment for a chat because I was becoming more and more scared for her well-being. I showed her a list of sex offenders within two miles of the apartment. I wanted her to recognize the dangers that were out in the world and as close as in our own neighborhood. I wanted her not put her put her life at risk by making bad choices. I was very surprised that there were 26 names on that list within two miles of the apartment.

However, Scott still had a major hold over Allison. In fact, the hold was so strong that, as the days went by, I could feel and see that Scott was brainwashing her. It seemed Scott was controlling her on such a high level that Allison was actually losing herself. It then came to a point when Scott and his friends were becoming more of a threat in my life in order to maintain a grip on my daughter. It then progressed to the stage where he was besieging her mind and not allowing her to contact me at all. Allison was basically being kidnapped and under complete mind control by Scott.

It became a crucial time for me to sit down and meditate and, in so doing, decide what I was going to do. I knew in my gut, since Scott wanted to keep Allison to himself, that there was some serious violence coming my way. People often wondered about how I would know what was going to happen before it happened, but it was an inner sense that I had since I was born, and my sense had proven to be one hundred percent correct. This gave me an advantage over Scott and his "army." I was not about to allow my daughter to stay with this man under these conditions any longer. I knew it was time for Allison and me to move on and get out of town. I had decided that our time in Salem was completely finished.

Unbeknownst to Scott, I was trained as an army cadet. The first thirteen years of my life was spent in a family of decorated marines who taught me how to look after myself. I was also trained in karate, surveillance, and I gained a great deal of experience on how to survive with my "street smarts." I am a very loving and caring human being and not violent in any way. However, this was my daughter and she had been kidnapped. I knew calling the police would do no good. I decided to personally take care of the situation. This is something I would not recommend to most people.

First, I donated or sold everything in the apartment. I then called my good friend, Grant, a Navy West Point decorated graduate. I asked him, "Grant, are you ready to do a rescue? My daughter has been kidnapped." Grant's reaction was immediate and quite staunch. He was vigorously excited by the idea. We found out that Allison had been held up in a little white shack just outside of town. It was approximately 1400 square feet with a front and back door and two windows in the front and two windows in the back. Allison was located in the back bedroom on the right hand side. Scott lived there with his parents. They had one large dog that was fortunately a docile pet. There were no gates or fences on the property. They had a big garden that was fifty yards from the main road. After Grant's parents realized what was going on with their son, Scott's parents gave me and Grant permission to enter the home and retrieve my daughter.

Two days later, at around six o'clock in the morning, Grant and I entered the house. In under one minute, I picked up Allison while she was sleeping and hurriedly carried her out to the back seat of my car, with Grant following close behind. We quickly sped out of town, heading towards Grant's home in Virginia Beach whicht was heavily protected by a military presence. Gratefully, we received a tip-off cell phone call from someone who found out that Scott and his crew were in pursuit of us.

To cap the climax, Scott failed to track down Grant and me. In the end, I learned that Scott had returned back to his home after falling short of finding the rescuers. In outrage and anger, he had trashed his home and severely beaten both of his parents. Prison was "calling," and that is where Scott landed.

When Grant and I arrived in Virginia Beach at the "Safe House", Allison had fully awoken by then. She was still under the influence of being brainwashed by Scott. Allison did not fully comprehend the dangers and risks of a totally controlled life with Scott. Not only was I was exhausted from this situation, I was still facing my own medical ordeals, in addition to having just completed a two year legal case where I was the consultant.

This was one of the biggest and messiest cases that I had ever encountered. It involved law firms, several companies, insurance companies, several individuals, and a federal agency. I had previously received a call in Salem from the attorney with the opposition notifying me that I had just won the case. The attorney made the personal phone call because he had just beaten one of the top law firms in the country.

The attorney was calling out of respect and recognition of my win. I was only a consultant and not an attorney.

A NEW LEAF TURNING

Understandably, I was exhausted. Allison was still going through repercussions of being out of control. After my consultation with her, I realized more emphatically that my job graduating her was complete and our life in Salem was definitely over. I had fought for my daughter and won. Allison graduated, despite a few family disasters and a kidnapping, and was time for Allison to go to college. My ex-wife, Desiree, married a Navy commander who worked for the Pentagon. He had gave Allison an opportunity to come and live with them and attend college.

I would never have agreed to this while Allison was growing up. At this juncture, the situation presented perfect timing. This was the excellent chance for Allison to have a secure life, away from the oppressive siege of Scott. Allison would be able to continue her education and be back with her mother and stepfather, who were doing very well and they both loved Allison. Navy discipline would provide sound and stable surroundings. Allison would live with Desiree and attend college. I went to England to Sally's house in order to address long needed medical attention. My plan was to leave the country for five months and then return to continue my business.

I had closed down everything in America and put all that was left into storage. I was happy that she was secure in going to college and that I was finally close to getting my medical cares sorted out. My gender issues were starting to increase to levels so high that I was dressing as a woman more and more. I managed to hold off these issues as much as I could while I was with Sally. I still wanted to live a life that society considered normal. I was at Sally's house living off the money that I had made before. We were quite content going out for dinner with friends, attending auctions, and being members of the country club.

There came news that the real estate market was climbing higher and higher. At the time, Sally owned quite a big house and we loved living there. I still had not gone for my medical help and I was silently suffering inside. I chose to put off this critical undertaking for the time being, not just because I was having a lot of fun, but I was focusing on getting Sally's daughter, Abby, into college. I was fearful about what my medical results might reveal. Sally and her friends were constantly asking me what was going on with the real estate market and what I thought they should do.

After I analyzed it all, I told Sally and her friends that the market was going to crash. I advised Sally and her friends that they drastically needed to sell their big houses and buy a small cottages in elite areas and put the left over money securely into their bank accounts. I also advised her friends who owned many rental properties, to sell them all and stash their investment capitol somewhere that would be secure. Sally's friends just laughed at the idea. Sally, however, followed my advice, though reluctantly, as she did not want to sell her big, beautiful home. She continued to follow my direction and she put her house on the market.

The house was sold within sixty days. Sally bought a modest cottage in Wymondon. Happily, through my advice, she received a nice, big discount. Consequently, she was able to place the rest of the funds safely inside a bank account. Nevertheless, Sally quickly became very upset over these decisions because her first home was continuing to go up in value. I tried to explain to her that she could not wait until the very last second. There would have been a higher risk that she could lose a great deal of money. It did not help that all the experts were saying that the market would not crash. Within two weeks, the market crashed bigger than it ever had. Sally, at this point, had made almost a half of a million dollars while her friend, who did not follow my advice, lost about $800,000.

I was doing very well working in a successful real estate business as an international real estate investor and consultant in America based in the United Kingdom. It was in 2003 that I decided to buy a Mercedes Benz. I received a big discount because I took a canceled customer order for a fully loaded blue car with beige interior. I liked the car, but I would have rather had another exterior color. It was a Mercedes Benz 200 convertible. My new friend, Devereaux, who I had recently met at the local pub, called that particular car a "powerless hair dryer." This pub was located across the street from Sally's new cottage.

Devereaux and I became extremely close friends. In fact, when we used to watch television together, it was a close and cuddly evening. We used to visit different places together and we would lounge at both his home and Sally's home, too. We would go shopping together and attend auctions. I felt like Devereaux and I had fallen in love with each other, although neither of us were gay. I had always been more like a woman and was sometimes dressing as one. The relationship seemed to be more of a man and woman relationship rather than that of a gay relationship.

Sally, on the other hand, was becoming more and more jealous, and rightfully so. Sally and I were an actual couple. The situation was crazy because on the inside, I was really a woman. Sally had a crush on Devereaux. He did not want to appear as "gay" by having affections toward me, so he covered it up by flirting with Sally. In the meantime, I was trying to be a man for Sally. This made me hold back my affection for Devereaux.

Devereaux used to stay at the house frequently. He did a lot of helpful things for us. I wanted to show my love toward Devereaux. I loved Devereaux and we had so many close moments together. Devereaux loved cars and he really started to like my Mercedes. I decided to give Devereaux my nearly new Mercedes Benz.

The Beginning of the End

I had been longing to show Devereaux who I really was and to explain why we had these close feelings together. This became the motivator for me to set out on a path to take care of all of the physical and gender problems that I had. I was still feeling quite ill most of the time. The first thing on my agenda was to finally find out what was wrong with me by going to a doctor. There was no question that my nervousness, dizziness, and feeling off-balance were becoming not only a lot worse, but unbearable. On top of that, I was beginning to have vision problems.

After finally going to a doctor, the doctor validated the fact that I had all these problems. He told me that it was a good thing that I had been externalizing them. Therefore, there was no medication that could help me. He said that if I had internalized these conditions, I would have needed medication. He suggested that my problems were a lot deeper and that I should visit a psychiatrist to find out the cause of these manifestations.

I made an appointment with the top psychiatrist in London with the hope to receive the best possible guidance. I arrived at his office and the psychiatrist asked me a series of questions. Then, the physician asked me if I had any questions and I responded with, "Yes, I want to know if I am mentally insane." The psychiatrist then said, "I want to try something with you." He proceeded to give me a shot in the arm of estrogen. Within a couple of minutes, he asked me how I felt. I had stopped shaking, my vision had improved, and I could instantly think clearly. Then, I replied, "I feel fantastic! What has been wrong with me?" The doctor replied, "You originally asked me if you were insane." The doctor pulled out a stack of charts and piled them on his desk and said, "Here is a stack of patients that have serious mental illnesses. You are not one of them. You are not insane and you do not have any kind of mental illness. Based on your entire medical history, you are simply a female. The testosterone that developed in your body since the early surgery is causing all of these issues. If you continue to live with these levels of testosterone in your body, it will eventually kill you. My treatment and plan for you is to stay on estrogen for two years and then to get gender surgery to reduce the high levels of testosterone to a normal female level. This will solve your medical issues. Other than a couple of medical follow-ups after surgery, you will be able to live a normal life without any further complications. I will give you a prescription for estrogen to keep you stable until your surgery."

I asked the doctor if he could have a second opinion. With a big smile on his face, he said, "Walk out that door and come back in, and I will tell you the same thing all over again." But, the doctor then, humorously, yet seriously said, "Because you have asked, I will recommend you to another psychiatrist in order to alleviate any worries. Because this was such a big, life changing decision, I made an appointment with another psychiatrist. I arrived at the doctor's office and he offered me a cup of tea, which I readily accepted. After he examined me and reviewed my complete medical history, the doctor agreed with the previous psychiatrist's diagnosis.

I left the doctor's office feeling really happy knowing that I was taking the right prescription for my condition. I did not feel crazy anymore for having the feelings of being a woman all of my life and, at times, dressing like one.

I walked down the street from the doctor's office, feeling both relieved and reinvigorated. The long awaited answer had been given. I went to the coffee shop around the corner to do some thinking. I could not believe how relaxed I felt and how clearly I was thinking. The biggest exhilaration was the fact that I was no longer shaking. It was such an enormous, joyous, and comforting alleviation from so much previous distress and affliction.

There was one big problem that I had not faced. I was with Sally and I was engaged to be married to her. In fact, the church had already been chosen and we had informed all of our friends. I remember the interview we had with the vicar of the church. I was told that we had to be accepted in order to be married in that church. That entailed being endorsed by the people of the village, as well as by the vicar himself. We found out a few days later that we had been accepted.

Three thoughts were going through my mind. First, I was really trying to love Sally. She was a beautiful lady that anyone would be happy to marry. However, I knew inside that I could not marry Sally because I felt like a woman. I tried my best to love her and carry on the life that we had together. I was secretly dealing with the reality and truth that I really wanted to be the bride, not the groom. Additionally, I was still feeling lost within myself and I thought that it could be related to my gender issues.

I was sitting in a coffee shop with all these realities and thoughts going through my mind. I knew that I had to go and see Sally to tell her all of these things. I also needed to tell her about the diagnosis. I told her that the doctor had put me on hormone therapy for two years, which was a requirement to have corrective surgery. After I told her all of this, she was very caring and supportive. She offered to help me in any way that she could. Obviously, the wedding was off. The very next morning, I took most of my male clothes and gave them to a charity shop. A few of the men's clothing items that were held back were for my transition purpose so folks in the village would not be confused or shocked. Then, I went on a marvelous shopping spree for my new female apparel. I purchased a wig that I used until my hair got longer. I also bought new makeup.

I returned home to Sally and she was crying. I knew, of course, what it was all about. I asked Sally, "Are you alright?" She stated that she had been speaking with her daughter, Anna. After Sally told Anna all the reasons she loved me, Anna responded with, "Mom, all of the things you love about David were female things, not male things." This made Sally cry heavy tears, as she realized that all of this time, she had essentially been in love with a woman. I consoled her by saying, "If I had been a man, you would have been a perfect and amazing wife for me!" My next remark to Sally was that I thought we both should be totally honest and admit that we were each in love with Devereaux. She looked up and smiled at me, speechless. I then said to her, "I look like a man right now because of all of the testosterone. I will not be having this transitional sugery for two years. Plus, it's going to take the same two years for the estrogen to kick in for my ultimate appearance to be like a girl.

I also told Sally that I thought she should choose to be with Devereaux. At this point, I could not proceed in pursuing the aspiring romance with Devereaux due to my upcoming transition. I told her that once I have transitioned, I would then like to explore the idea of being with Devereaux. I told Sally that if it was to occur that Devereaux was to fall in love with her in the meantime, then I would walk away. Sally agreed.

I asked Sally if I could still stay at the cottage until this change in life happened. She thoughtfully said, "Yes." Everything became agreed upon and arranged. At this point in time, I was on female hormones and dressing mostly as a woman. At the age of 42, David no longer existed. Sally must have realized that her time with me was more like living with a teenage girl. She was dressing me up in very beautiful clothes, too.

There were times when I used to go to weekly meetings regarding gender transition. All of the other girls would get changed at the meeting, and then get changed back into male apparel after the meetings. One day, I pulled up in front of the building for a meeting and got out of my vehicle wearing high heels, a skirt, and holding a bag of chips. One of the girls shouted, "How did you get those chips, girl?" I replied, "I got them from the Chip Shop on my way here!" At that moment, that girl looked terrified and ran into the meeting in session and said, "Look at her! She got some chips dressed as a woman!"

Later the group told me that I could not do that and that I had to transition more slowly, as it was too dangerous to do otherwise. It was at this moment that I realized that I was already a girl. I looked like one and nobody paid any attention to the difference. Looking back, I felt so natural as a girl in every respect, especially with regards to having a female brain. The change for me was automatically instant. As soon as I took the rest of my clothes to the charity shop, I considered myself a woman from that point forward.

This episode was way ahead of everybody else in the group. I was told that I was different; just like a regular, beautiful girl. They said, "We are not like you. It's going to take us each a lot longer, if ever." I sadly understood that there were a lot of diverse types of people transitioning. It was not a "one size fits all" scenario. For example, I was immediately like a normal woman. Within six months, my breasts had grown, my skin was soft, and I did not have much hair on my body. I did not need any facial surgery or other enhancements to look more like a woman. I was basically a female from day one. I just needed to have the corrective genital surgery. Since I had surgery as a young boy, this proposed new surgery would probably be quite an easy, yet long, procedure as I already had some female genital components.

A NEW SELF, A NEW SPECULATION

I went on to live my life happily as a woman. I faithfully continued to attend these meetings once a week for two years. It was great, as I made a lot of friends. We had lots of laughs and did wild and crazy things together. Hanging out all over town in Nottingham in the United Kingdom for about two years were some of the most amazing times of my life. During this time, I still cared deeply for Devereaux. At that time, I believed that I wanted to be with Devereaux.

Finally, having surgery was a very happy decision and a wonderful moment in my life. I was finally the gender that I knew I was supposed to be since I was a child. Everything fit and was natural. Unlike the other way, when I was always working very hard just to function. My transition fit well with people that I knew, too. They liked being around me and felt pleasant in my presence. Men who were straight often liked the previous David and did not understand, as they were definitely not gay. It was extremely confusing for everyone involved, but now the world seemed quite normal. I felt as if all the planets were aligned properly.

I was still living at Sally's house when Devereaux and Sally had started dating. I used to playfully tease Devereaux a bit, but Sally did not like that. She would not allow me to be around Devereaux unless she was present. The three of us continued to socialize together. We enjoyed going out for food and drinks. There is no doubt that these were all truly precious times together.

I decided to start a new business. It was a business for women and was located just down the road from Sally's home. There was a vacant shop open at the windmill. It was particularly quaint. I rented the space. It felt comfortable and it was located next to a friend's shop that I knew well. I came up with the unique business name of "Love U Gifts." I had a special logo designed. It was really a lovely design; red letters with surrounding hearts.

I was so excited about this new venture that I flung the doors open for all to come and see, though I still needed merchandise. I did something one should never do as a brand new female owner who felt like a teenage girl full of dreams who wants to open a gift shop. I went to an international wholesale product convention with my checkbook. Within two days, I had purchased over $75,000 in merchandise. It was the most incredible shopping spree of a lifetime.

The only problem was that I had bought so much stock that it totally packed my new shop with hardly any room to walk. Looking back now, there are three key principles that I should have known before opening a new retail shop.

First, only place a few items of the same product at a time in the shop, and place them neatly in an organized fashion so not to confuse customers when they walk in. Customers do not need to face a barrage of merchandise because it turns them off to buy anything.

Second, only buy a bit of each wholesale item in order to find out if and/or how well they sell.

Third, do not buy merchandise that you like. Buy things that customers in general would like to buy.

Even though it turned out to be a fun business to run, in reality, I wound up with enough Christmas presents for the rest of my life. The good thing about operating the shop was that so many of the folks in the village had the chance to see the new me. Fortunately, I never lost any friends. People told me that I was more suited to be this way. I truly have very loving, caring, and understanding friendships which I have maintained until this day. I maintained my residence at Sally's while running my establishment. I was beginning to live a normal life and understood the meaning of it. I believe so many people take that for granted.

INTO HER OWN

I continued to run the shop for a little more than a year. Since the time was drawing closer to the time for my corrective surgery and the shop was not really making much money, I decided to close it down. I maintained my friends at Windmill, where the shop was located, and then started making plans with Sally and Devereaux for all of our futures.

The crazy fact of the matter was that I was with Sally, but I had feelings for Devereaux. Sally decided that she could no longer be in a relationship with me because I was truly a woman. Deep down, Sally really wanted to be with Devereaux.

A few days later, I had a conversation with Sally about me moving to another home of my own in Oakham, Rutland, which was just a few miles away. I needed my own place to go to while recovering from my operation. Also, Devereaux would then be able to move in with Sally, which is exactly what happened. In the process, Devereaux helped me move everything I owned into my new home. He even delivered and put together my new brass bed that I had purchased. From the very beginning of this move, I really missed him.

Next, I flew to Thailand to receive my transitional/corrective surgery. The surgery took place on October 28, 2005 at Aikchol Hospital in Chonburi, Thailand. I chose the most qualified and also the most expensive surgeon in the world to perform this delicate procedure. Since I had a prior similar operation as a child, though for opposite results, this made the new surgery much more dangerous and complicated. I still had female organs that had not been removed. The compelling job of this surgeon was to turn me back into the true female that I had always been. This was not a simple male to female inversion technique surgery. My surgery was much more complex.

The pre-consultation with the surgeon was easy and simple because all of the many forms that I signed regarding the risks were never read by me. I was too terrified. I remember saying to the doctor, "I'm either going to wake up back here or in heaven." I had a pretty sound sleep the night before. I had a prior visit from my friend, Miles. He was in Thailand looking after a friend from America. I had met him in the doctor's office and he was attracted to me.

The next thing that I remembered was being carted down to the surgery room and being asked by the doctor, "How are you?" The next thing I recall was waking up in the surgery room and asking myself, "Am I alive or dead?" When I realized that I was truly alive and kicking, I made a quick look "down there," and consequently passed out! The very next memory was waking up again and seeing Miles standing over me with a big smile. He was holding two dozen beautiful red roses. As it turned out, he had traveled all over the place trying to find them.

During my two week long duration of recovery in the hospital, Miles stood by my side the whole time, along with Merin, who traveled with

151

me from England to Thailand. We were scheduled to have our surgeries at the same time. Merin had many difficulties after her surgery and came close to dying several times. She was in the opposite room from me. It was very scary, as I was hearing about her complications. I could not do anything about it. Merin and I both desired to heal together in the hospital.

Fortunately, the hospital worked it out. They moved two beds together in the same room. We held each other's hands. I was crying because I was afraid that Merin might die. I was also scared for myself. Merin was equally comforting me. The doctor entered our room and said, "You were born to be a woman, and your medical records show it." He advised me that now my mind, heart, and body were all in sync with each other and that everything would be fine. He was right.

The good news about Merin was that she came out of danger, and we were both heading for a fast recovery. My recovery from this advanced surgical procedure took only two weeks. Merin and I were released and transferred back to the hotel for further recovery. We were monitored by the doctors and nurses there. The care given to us was absolutely outstanding. I remember one time when I could not urinate because my urethra was so swollen. I had to be rushed to the doctor to rectify the problem. I was terrified. I worried that my bladder might explode. Thankfully, it did not and I was alright.

Miles was indeed a wonderful, sweet gentleman who looked after me religiously while we were in Thailand together. I remember after leaving the hospital, and thus being in the hotel recovering, he brought more roses to me. Reflecting back, I think it was quite comical that Miles was trying to be my boyfriend while I was recovering from my surgery.

We continued to spend time together the whole time I was in Thailand. He took me out and showed me some of the most marvelous highlights of Thailand. We remained friends long after I returned to England with Merin. Departing from Miles was incredibly emotional. I gave him a kiss at the hotel and said that they should have their big goodbye there rather than at the airport. It would have been too hard on the both of us otherwise.

Merin and I left for the airport. As we were going through the gate on the way to the plane, I heard Miles shouting, "I love you. I love you!" Miles was on the other side of the gate. Although we had agreed to say our goodbyes at the hotel, Miles rushed to the airport to say farewell.

I looked over at Merin, while walking to board the plane, and said, "He's a lovely man, but I still love Devereaux."

HOME AGAIN, HOME AGAIN

The journey in flight was very uncomfortable. We had to sit dealing with post-surgery discomfort for so long. Upon arrival at London Heathrow airport, Merin took her car home to London and I took my vehicle to Oakham in Rutland. By this time, Sally and Devereaux had already organized and prepared my new home for me. It was a fantastic homecoming. I settled in nicely and launched into a happy pattern of cooking meals for friends. It was great. I used to walk into town, shop at the market, socialize at the country club, and pay visits to friends. I was still on the voyage of visiting auctions and traveling down to Nottingham to support others in transition. I was fully transitioned, felt fulfilled, and desired to help people. There were three outside personal matters going on at the same time. The first one, of course, was the issue of Devereaux. The second was the issue of Miles. The third was the issue of Merin.

Dealing with Miles was the easiest. We stayed in contact as friends for quite a long time. The romance with him was a whirlwind romance only. It was not in the cards for us to ever be together. I loved Miles as a dear friend. Through the yeaars, he seemed to get over his feelings for me.

The next issue was Devereaux. There was already the decisive agreement that had been made between Sally, Devereaux, and myself. Sally and Devereaux would be together in the same cottage that I was originally in with Sally. Devereaux, in a sense, had taken my place. After I returned from surgery, I discovered that Sally would not allow me to see Devereaux alone. Sally was making every effort to ultimately marry Devereaux. However, Sally and I still maintained our friendship and we continued call one another and occasionally lunched.

I learned that Devereaux was starting to suffer from bipolar disorder. Devereaux could be really hyper and productive, and other times, due to depression, he would sleep for weeks. I asked Sally if I could see Devereaux on several occasions, but I was not allowed. I continued to live in my little house, wondering if Devereaux desired to see me. I truly believed that he did.

Although I did not see it coming, Merin was falling in love with me. I had stayed in contact with Merin two or three times a week. She would sometimes came over to my place for dinner. One night, when Merin came over for dinner, she asked if the two of us could live together as a couple. She wanted me to move into her house in London. Yet, after Merin coaxed me several times, I reluctantly obliged. My reasoning for this was not just in loyalty to Merin since she had done so much for me, but I needed to get away from Sally and Devereaux. It was a confusing triangle that needed to stop.

On another note, I still had friends and wanted to do right by them. One of my friends had recently died because of post-surgery complications. Another good friend of mine became depressed from constant bullying and committed suicide by jumping in front of an oncoming train. A third friend, whom I used to visit often, died of a brain tumor three weeks after a Christmas party. I was present at that party to support her and to be with her friends. I vividly recall singing, "I Love Christmas Day" to her at this event. I sang my heart out for her. Everything had changed. It was time to move on. I accepted Merin's proposition. The move to London was on its way.

UTTER GRIEF, TOTAL DESPAIR

All through this time, I still had my dog, Buffy. He had been with me through all the years of raising Allison. He was over eighteen years old. I had flown him over from America to England to live out his days as a retired king. In those days, to fly a dog across the ocean would cost about $8,500. I would have paid $100,000, if necessary. Buffy and I were living at Merin's and, for the time being, it was quite a pleasant time. Merin and I did many fun things together. Yet, the fact remained that I was not in love with Merin. This was weighing heavily on my thoughts. Quite often, I used to go out to the country, sit down and contemplate about what I had done with respect to my moving in with Merin. On top of this, Buffy was not doing well during the last days of his life. I had no other choice but to have Buffy put to sleep. It was the hardest thing that ever played on my mind, even today. Merin was fully supportive in this whole very sad event.

Just a few days before Buffy went to doggie heaven, I received a call from Sally. I thought it was about Devereaux's birthday. I had some presents in the back of my car and I wanted Sally to give them to Devereaux. Next, Sally said, "Devereaux's dead. He died in a car crash on his way to your house." I screamed at the top of my lungs, "No, no, not Devereaux! This cannot be true!" I must have said that a hundred times. Then, I desperately proclaimed to Sally, "You were supposed to look after him!" Sally hung up. I succumbed to an onslaught of weeping and constant crying, repeating the words, "No, not Devereaux! It cannot be!"

I had just lost someone that I loved deeply and it changed me forever. In spite of it all, moving in a space and time of complete devastation, shock and sorrow, I finally got up from my crying spot on the front lawn and walked into the house to tell Merin what had happened. Sadly, and to my shock, Merin's reception was not so consoling. In subsequent days, Merin and I gradually grew apart. Merin became consistently controlling. I could hardly leave the house without a major report of where I was going.

Two days later, Sally informed me that, prior to Devereaux's death, they had gotten into a fight due to one of Devereaux's hyperactive moods which was attributed to his bipolar disorder. As a result, Devereaux had jumped into his car and had driven off towards my home. I learned that the police had notified Sally with the news that Devereaux had died instantly in a car crash.

I found myself sitting at the accident scene holding pieces of the car that Devereaux had died in. I also left his presents in the back of my car where I had originally placed them to surprise him on his birthday. I left them there for over two months until I was strong and capable enough to remove them.

Soon after this tragedy, I was contacted by Devereaux's mother. She had read a post that I had written about Devereaux on his memorial website. She invited me to visit her and we soon became natural friends..

Subsequently, I helped and supported Devereaux's mother by doing all sorts of jobs and duties, including moving her furniture, doing shopping, and other tasks. In an emotional moment, she gave me one of Devereaux's sweatshirts. I kept it devotedly until one day in the future, I realized it was not healthy for me to keep it any longer.

It was obvious that Devereaux's mother became worried about me because I was increasingly becoming more and more depressed. Nevertheless, I pushed forward with my life and stayed friends with his mother. This tremendous and heartbreaking event had a tremendous impact on my life. It took five years for me to come to terms with the reality of his death.

It was becoming more and more apparent that I needed to escape from the grips of Merin due to her dominance, and the loss of Devereaux. It got so bad with Merin that I moved out of the house and into my own apartment with the help of my friends. I moved to a flat about seven miles away. I kept the friends that I had already made and maintained a distant friendship with Merin.

Merin eventually fell in love with a wonderful man. They got married and moved away to another city together.

A NEW PAGE TURNS AND FLIPS

I kept busy in the new flat. It took some time, but I made the apartment beautiful. I used to entertain my old friends that I had met previously, and also with new ones, too. I was still suffering greatly from what had happened with Merin, the death of my dog, Buffy, and the death of Devereaux. In the outcome, I made the most of my pain by making this flat and myself as put-together, and presentable as possible.

When I was out one day, I met a man named Alvin. We had known each other before through association with mutual friends. We started dating for a bit. I used to look after his daughter in the flat. In a way, we became like a little family. He was a perfect gentleman and took me out often. We had beautiful evenings together. Then, one day, I asked him what he did for a living, and he responded with, "I just take care of business when I need to." He made it clear that he had planned for the two of us to move in together. In my mind, I realized that he was a gangster and it was this realization that made me want to get out of the relationship. Alvin's lifestyle, on top of the post- traumatic stress that I was enduring, caused the relationship to end.

About three weeks later, I met Penn. He lived about four doors down from me. Penn had a son and we quickly became a unit together. We did all of the usual activities; having movie nights at home, visiting Penn's parents, and dining at restaurants.

160

Once, Penn's father was giving me a tour of his home. He showed me into the living room and said, "What do you think about this room?" I said, "Well, once you decorate it and get some new furniture, it will be nice!" I thought that he was asking for my advice as far as what to do with the room. As it turned out, he had just finished redecorating it. This was such an awkward moment and it did not go well. Anyway, none of that really mattered since Penn was really a jerk at times. I ended up leaving him. The only thing that I missed about Penn was cuddling with him.

I continued to hang-out with my friends. On the way home one day, I pulled into a filling station and filled up my car with petrol. As I was standing in line, I noticed this attractive man in front of me. I had this weird sense of connection with him. As he was paying for his petrol, he turned around, smiled at me, and then told the cashier to please pay for "this beautiful lady's petrol, as well." I was astonished and rejected his offer, but he paid for it anyway. He proceeded to give me his name, phone number, and address, and said, "Please call me and I will cook you dinner." After another big smile, he went off on his way.

I felt so astounded and sensed some sort of déjà vu experience. It was risky, but I felt that I had to call him. His name was Denver. I called Denver and he made a date for us to have dinner at his house. About a week later, I arrived at Denver's home and he let me in. His home was a complete disaster. It drastically needed major renovations. There was not even any drywall. The one room that he lived in was reasonable in comparison.

During and after dinner, he kept telling me that I was beautiful. His eyes were very alluring, too. After our romantic dinner, he said, "Please look into my eyes. I need to tell you something. I feel very suicidal." I was deeply astounded and said, "I want to help you live."

Denver went onto say, "My mom and father died, I lost my job, I am an alcoholic, and am almost flat broke. Also, my house is seven months behind in payments." I responded with, "Denver, I cannot believe you put me in this position. I need to really think about what I am going to do about this predicament. I certainly know that I am going to provide you with emotional support. I cannot leave you in this condition, knowing if you did kill yourself, I would not be able to live with myself." I could tell that this man was very serious regarding his intentions. The problem on my side was that I was already exhausted with everything that I had been through. I made Denver promise me that he would not do anything until I returned. He agreed.

While driving home in my car, I asked God, "Why, me? Why do I always end up in these situations?" I quickly realized that this free petrol that I had received was about to get quite expensive. I wrote down an overall plan to help Denver recover. I knew a lot about survival and human nature. Also, I had a strong instinct that Denver could, indeed, kill himself. If he did not kill himself, I felt he could accidentally be killed. Denver was walking at least eight miles each week completely drunk on a very dangerous stretch of road. I was able to obtain this information because of the questions I had asked him when we first met. The option for neighbors to help him was no good at all. They limited their help;

bringing food and furniture. None of them had any idea how serious this whole dilemma truly was.

I had two choices. First, walk away and see what happens, or secondly, just help him. I truly felt some weird connection with him. Additionally, we had already been intimate together. I realized that I had become both emotionally and physically attached to Denver. I was a real estate investor as well, so I could see myself helping Denver get a good deal on a house. At the time, I did not realize that Denver had fallen in love with me so quickly. Therefore, helping him out of troubles on this level would ultimately make life a lot more complicated for both of us.

BIG PLAN

I first came to realize that Denver was a spoiled brat. On the other hand, so was I. First, I realized that I needed to help make Denver stable. Then, I needed to keep him busy so he would not think about killing himself. So, while we continued to date, I included myself within the plan to be with him.

I truly believed that Denver was not a depressed person, nor was he trying to kill himself because of some sort of medical mental disorder. He seemed to be a guy who simply got himself into some deep trouble and was unable to get himself out of it. The only plan that he could think of was to end his life. Of course, alcohol played a major role in this. He was also very handsome and dynamic. The amount of alcohol that he was drinking was causing his good looks to go downhill fast.

I thoroughly explained to him what my plan of action was in order to see if he agreed with it. I told him that I would stay with him as his girlfriend. The next thing on the agenda was to put the house up for sale. We would move to where he always dreamed of living, as long as it was near a safe town that he could walk to and where he would be in no danger. Most people would think that that kind of place would be something like Hawaii. Denver had his mind set on being in St. Petersburg, England which was about eighty miles away. I agreed with him about moving there. I felt it would be an adventure. I also thought we may have a chance of having a good relationship if he could get out of this mess. I would also be helping him save his life. As I look back at this whole situation, I realize that I should have prayed with him after the moment he informed me that he was suicidal.

On the other side of the coin, I realized that this whole plan was completely insane up to this point. In facing reality, I explained to him that all of this would cost a pretty penny. I felt that I could not leave him there to die. I knew I would not be able to handle it if he killed himself. Additionally, I was looking at the possibility of the two of us becoming a good couple.

In the midst of all of this, Denver got on his knees and proposed to me. He said something very odd after the proposal. He told me it was very important that I keep my legs beautiful with no blemishes. The ring that he proposed to me with was one from the past. It was a gorgeous, Tiffany, 2 karat diamond ring. It was the only item that Denver had left that had any value. The ring fit me perfectly. Denver looked up at me and said, "This is for you, my beautiful princess!"

Our agreed plan to get Denver out of trouble was going to cost between twenty-five and thirty thousand United Kingdom pounds. I also told Denver that I would make-up for all of the mortgage payments so his house would not go into foreclosure. Denver had the extreme desire to eventually move away because of all of his bad memories.

He wanted to move into a nice apartment in St. Petersburg, England. I told Denver that we needed to put the house on the market. Next, I explained that after his house was sold, he would need to reimburse me for the money that I had spent on this endeavor. He went along with that. Hence, happily engaged, we packed our bags and moved to St. Petersburg. As I projected, we found a nice apartment that had an easy walking distance for Denver to get into town. It was also near a river with ducks. This was a perfect spot where Denver could sit and feed the ducks while he continued to recover from his ordeal. He had stopped drinking and had developed into a happy, loving fiancée. He even found employment in town.

OUT FROM UNDER

Everything was progressing beautifully, and my plan to save Denver appeared to be a great success. There was one thing that I did not know. I was beginning to find out that Denver was an extremely controlling man. For example, the statement that he made to me about keeping my legs blemish free gave me the creeps. I came to discover that it was not just about that, but it was about everything in the whole picture. He was trying to control the way I dressed and how I behaved. He made it clear that I belonged to him and could never leave his side.

This was a big problem for me. I was paying for everything, and I needed to do my work. This meant that I had to go out of town a lot, and I did. Upon many returns, he became extremely angry with me. His behavior was so bad that I had to call the police. They advised me that this situation was out of control. The best solution would be for me to leave and go as far away as possible to get away from him.

I took their advice and decided to move back into the old house until it was sold. Nonetheless, I continued to send Denver money until the time arrived when he was able to support himself, and also get assistance from the government to pay for things such as rent and food. This whole ordeal was extremely distressing for me because I cared deeply for him, too. His bad temper and ruling nature were just too much for me to bear.

Denver was happy that I was living in the old house. I stayed in contact with him by phone. As long as he believed that I was not seeing anyone else, he was alright with that. He promised to get counseling with the hope that we could eventually live with one another again.

There was another big problem that was arising. The police from different counties were knocking on my door. The neighbors who had failed to help Denver were out to attack me. They told the police that I was not supposed to be staying in that house without Denver there. The police checked everything and realized that the information that I gave to them was the truth.

One of the neighbors had a plan to buy Denver's house at a cheap price for one of their relatives. They actually were hoping that Denver would fail and lose his home. They did not like me being in the picture because I was helping him. It was not too long before I received a full offer for his home. I called Denver and told him that, if we sold the house to the potential buyer, we would make 60,000 pounds, which is equivalent to $81,186.36 United States dollars.

Denver surprised me by saying, "Don't give me any money. You keep the money because I will use it again for alcohol and die. My life is happy now with what I do receive and I do not need anything extra." He then asked, "After you sell the house, will you come back home?" I said, "I will consider it." I also told him that I did not want his portion of the money. I was planning to put his portion in the bank and send him little checks over a period of time until the balance reached zero.

Denver did not want that. He did not want any money at all. He was pleased with the money that he was already receiving and did not want to get any more for two reasons. First of all, he might start drinking again. The main reason was that he would ultimately lose his government benefits if he received any extra income.

I was distraught by all of this. It was a bad relationship and I did not want to keep his portion of the money on the house. Next, I delayed the sale of the house. In doing this, I was able to think about the whole situation. I wanted to get the $30,000 back that I had already spent, but did not want to spend his money. Also, I would have to pickup Denver from his home in St. Petersburg and bring him to the closing. That would also be a very stressful situation.

In any account, while I was waiting to make a decision, and while delaying the closing, fate stepped in and the real estate market crashed overnight. This reduced the house value by 80,000 UK pounds. This made the buyer back out of the deal. Thus, I was 20,000 UK pounds in negative equity.

I was happy about all of this for some strange reason. I had just lost 30,000 UK pounds, but was free from Denver's controlling dominance. Now, I did not have to deal with Denver's money nor feel guilty by keeping it. I made the decision to let the house go into foreclosure. That meant that I could stay in the house for over a year without paying mortgage payments. This decision would help regain at least some of the money.

I called Denver by phone and told him what had happened. He was not angry about the money, but he was very upset that I was going to remain in the house and not return to him. Due to his fury, I knew that I could never go back to him. I had done my job because Denver was alright now.

PAXTON

I continued to live my life in the house and was continuously emotionally attacked by a few of our neighbors. I had a few friends, so it was not that bad. Several months down the road, I met a man named Paxton. He knew of me through a mutual friend, Patrick. At this time, I was single and living alone. Paxton enticed me with a tasty steak dinner at the local pub. I accepted his informal dinner invitation. We had a wonderful evening and decided we wanted to begin dating each other.

A few weeks later, Paxton moved in with me. He felt this need to protect me. We were beginning to have a nice life together. We shared lots of fun, laughter, as well as making many new friends.

Paxton's mother was in a nursing home and we would visit her every Saturday. We would take her shopping downtown and eat in a quaint restaurant. We spent lots of time talking and laughing with Paxton's mom at the nursing facility. His mom was in her eighties. She had heart problems, diabetes, and subsequent loss of both of her legs. She was a wonderful, precious lady that developed a loving relationship with me. She treated me as though I was her daughter-in-law.

My life at this time was quite stable, despite periodic phone calls from Denver in a drunken rage. I was still missing my dog, Buffy. This made Paxton and I decide to get another dog. We both realized that a shih tzu canine would be the perfect fit, as I had always thought about how much fun it would be to have one.

Normally, I would go and check out the animal shelter for a dog. I had always been a big animal shelter supporter. My foundation donates money to causes for animal welfare on an annual basis. Instead, I chose to look inside a newspaper about dogs for sale. The reason I made this decision was because I knew that I could not find this type of dog in an animal shelter, or it would have been very hard. The great thing about finding a dog in a dog newspaper is that many of them are being sold because they cannot be looked after any longer due to many circumstances. Many times, these are pre-animal shelter dogs.

Paxton and I were sifting through the dog newspaper and we discovered that there were hundreds of dogs of this type for sale. In a way, I felt guilty as I did not want to pick out the prettiest one and leave all the others behind without knowing more about them. I decided to pick out the one listing that had no photo at all. Interestingly, all of the other dogs with pictures were selling for anywhere between 1500 and 3000 pounds. There was one pup that had no photo and was going for 200 pounds. The listing further said that this particular shih tzu had been returned three times because of its aggressive habit of chasing cats. The owner was feeling desperate since she was having to keep the dog in a small cage, outside, and in all kinds of weather conditions.

I looked at Paxton and emphatically declared, "We are going to rescue this little shih tzu!" He nodded and happily agreed. Then, we found out that this little "cat snatcher" was living 250 miles away.

We hustled off to the ATM machine to capture the cash. Then we pursued our five hundred mile roundtrip journey to pick up this lucky dog.

Right before we made our arrival at the dog owner's home, we called to let the lady know that we were almost there. She said, "Oh, no! That's my friend's house. I will meet you at the service station." They arrived and there was the dog sitting in the back seat of the car with no leash, no collar, nor any toys. The pup had nothing. I asked the woman if she had any papers on the dog, and she said that she would mail them to me. I then asked if the dog, which was a boy, had a name, and she replied, "His name is Quaver. He was named after the crisps that he loves to eat." She asked me if I liked Quaver and I replied, "I love him!" The woman then proclaimed, "Good, because you can't bring him back because that would be the fourth time. I shook my head and agreed.

The lady offered to put Quaver into my car because the dog could get frightened and possibly become aggressive. At that moment, the dog looked at the previous owner and immediately pounced into my arms and started licking my face. This dog knew exactly what owner he wanted. The woman started crying. I gave her a hug and said goodbye.

So, there we were with a beautiful black dog that hated cats. The reason that Paxton stayed sitting in the car was because I had told him that the dog did not like cats or men and that he needed to get used to Paxton. Well, as soon as Quaver was placed in the back seat of my car, he jumped into the front seat onto Paxton's lap, licking his face profusely. Quaver stayed there all of the way home. Paxton looked at me and said, "So, this dog doesn't like men?" I gave Paxton a wicked smile.

I really wanted to have a light brown dog, but this black one was alright. After a few stops on the way home to use the bathroom, we finally made it back. The first thing we did upon arriving home was to take Quaver to a groomer and have him bathed and groomed. When we picked him up from the groomers, we found that Quaver was a stunning mix of a light brown and white dog. We realized that Quaver only appeared black because of the accumulation of dirt on his body. It became a happy note that Quaver made a wonderful addition to the family. On an extra nice note, Paxton's mother, Beatrice, absolutely loved Quaver and Quaver helped make major improvements to her health.

BACK AND FORTH

Paxton, Quaver, and I continued to live as a family. Next, relationship issues started to crop up. I had been through too much by that time to join hands with him. Since I had no desire to marry at that time, Paxton and I split up. After our breakup, I did well. As a matter of fact, I did not feel sad. Then, a few weeks later, I met Santino, and it was a whirlwind romance. I met him online. Our first date was in a restaurant and he was the most handsome man that I had ever seen. He took my hand and wined and dined me like I had never undergone before. I was lavished in red roses on a constant basis. He always took me out to the most lavish places. He also took me to meet his family. Over time, our relationship seemed perfect.

One Saturday night in a lavish, upscale restaurant, he got on his knees and proposed marriage by placing an engagement ring on my finger. I looked at him lovingly and said, "Yes!" Next, I ended up moving in with Santino. Life seemed very good and loving. That was until one day that I discovered that Santino was not who he claimed to be. He had abandoned his wife and three children. He had a criminal past. I figured all this out because I put my investigative background to use and discovered who he really was.

On a trip down to visit one of his cousins, I finally conjectured that I just could not live with these lies anymore. I confronted him on this trip and explained that I was actually leaving him there at his cousin's house. Next, I ran to my car and drove off at a high speed to gather my things. I remember after loading the last of my bits in the car, this girl behind me was shouting out, "I've been there, baby! You leave that liar!"

In the meantime, Paxton had been constantly calling and asking me to come back home to him. I finally agreed. Upon arrival back home to Paxton, we really did not talk about our previous breakup. We just got on with our lives as always had. We continued the pattern of going to visit Paxton's mom, and unfortunately, she was getting worse. Also, the house was about a month away from foreclosure. It was time to make some very serious decisions.

After a comprehensive conversation with Paxton, he expressed his real dream of moving to Wales. I asked him about his current job and the seniority and benefits that he would be losing should he move. He responded that after his mom died, he wanted to just scratch it all and start a new life in Wales. I knew that he simply could not afford to make a giant move like this. The words of his mother kept haunting me. She said, "As long as my Paxton is with you, I know he will be alright after I'm gone." At that time, I did not have the heart to tell her that I did not truly love him in the way that I should. Looking back now, I doubt if I ever dated a man as good as Paxton.

I made some phone calls to a few friends and colleagues and was able to find a bungalow in Wales that was not too far from the ocean. When I broke the good news, Paxton was ecstatically happy. We both agreed that I would go down to the new home and get everything ready. As part of this agreement, I would return on weekends to see Paxton and his mother. After Paxton's one-month notice given to his employer, he would then move down to Wales and be with me. Next, we would both travel to visit Paxton's mother every weekend. It was four hundred miles, round trip.

Sadly, during the final days that Paxton could stay at the old house before it went into foreclosure, and also during his final days at work, his mom passed on. Fortunately, Paxton had the fulfillment of seeing his mother one last time before she died. It was on a Friday night when I was in Wales making preparations on the new house. I feel sad to this day that I never had the chance to say goodbye to her.

Next, Paxton came home to Wales and we planned his mother's funeral together. I created a beautiful and comfortable home for us and Quaver. At least Paxton was living where he had always dreamed to be. Happily, Paxton found a new job within two weeks and we were very content again. We bought two bikes and a car. We regularly took Quaver to the beach and had great fun. There were times when we would ride our bikes as far as 25 miles away. We lived the free and happy beach lifestyle. We also enjoyed seeing our friends, shopping, and going to restaurants. It was truly an amazing and satisfying lifestyle.

We had no idea what the future had in store for us. It was obvious now that my gender issues had long vanished and was a thing of the past. I was just like anyone else, but I still had long lost dreams of becoming a singer.

In 2011, I chose the stage name "Elainee," (pronounced e-lane-e). I started singing Cliff Richard's songs, such as "Living Doll, Theme for a Dream, The Young Ones, and Traveling Light." He was my favorite singer since I was a teenager. It was a wonderful, fulfilling experience for me, just living out my dreams. I packed venues and was told that I was on my way to stardom by industry leaders.

Along the way, I realized that my creativity stretched further than cover songs. I began to write my own songs and searched for new songs by other songwriters. I went to work online to search for gifted songwriters. I placed a notice on LinkedIn via the "Songwriting Industry" grouping, stating that I was a singer in England looking for original songs to perform. Irene Leland, who lived in St. Louis, Missouri, found the posting and responded right away. Irene sent me two of her songs. In June of 2012, Irene and I decided to collaborate on music projects together and developed a treasured friendship.

Irene and I spoke on the phone and realized that we could create some wonderful music together. I was very interested in signing-on Irene's songs. In satisfaction and gradual development, Irene continued to send along more of her originals, which I felt had great potential. A mutual agreement transpired for Irene and I to co-sign ten of Irene's folk/pop songs on an equal publishing deal. Irene was going to be the songwriter and I would perform them.

AWAKENING IN TRUTH

I lived in a little bungalow on 34 Regent Road in Rhyl, North Wales. I had been searching for something my whole life. However, there was a truth that was about to unfold and set me free forever.

I was a lost child growing up. I distinctly remember looking over the motorway bridge and watching cars roll off into the distance. I used to say to myself, "I don't belong here." I knew in a deep sense that somewhere down that road was where I was meant to be. I consciously thought it was kind of strange thinking this at the time. I was actually a really happy kid. Additionally, I had many other spiritual happenings that occurred to me as the future moved on.

There were strange situations where people would stop me on the street when I was a child and tell me that I was a special. I remember one significant moment as a child when I went to church on my own. It was on a day when no one was there. I was kneeling at the altar in deep thought and prayer when, suddenly, I felt a strong awareness of being surrounded by a force of comforting protection. Then, I heard the glorious sound of singing.

Upon opening my eyes and looking in front of me, I saw three tall, white, magnificent angels standing together in a row before the altar. It was their voices that were singing. I was immediately enveloped in a tranquilizing and revitalizing immersion. At the same time, I felt an overwhelmingly frightened reaction. I jumped up and quickly raced down the church aisle and ran away. I ended up coming back, not long afterwards, to discover that everything was normal again inside the church.

Throughout my teenage years, the closeness with my biological father, Elvis Presley, was extremely strong. It was nothing at all like being a fan with regard to his music. It was something very deep inside of both father and child, a natural connection. It was so deep that I knew when my father was in grave danger. I made a phone call at age thirteen to him in an attempt to save his life. It was from a child's point of view as to why this powerful link existed.

I was feeling frightened for Elvis and his health, about four years before his death. I was with my friend, William, when I made the call to Elvis from inside the phone box, just outside of St. Peter's School in Coggeshall. The phone boxes in those days had an A and B button. You were supposed to push one of those buttons in order to get in touch with the operator after dialing "O", after which you inserted the coins. I never had much change and I was concerned that I would not get through or have enough time to talk.

Surprisingly, the phone rang and a man answered. I said, "Can I speak with Elvis Presley, please?" He said, "Who are you and where are you calling from?" I said, "I am David from Coggeshall, England." He said, "Wait a minute." Then, Elvis came to the phone. I said, "Hello, I don't have much time on this call, but I am worried about you." Elvis said,

"Don't worry about me. I'm alright." I then, said, "But, I am..."
Knowingly, at that second, Elvis responded with, "Just live your life and
be happy. I will be there for you when you need me." Next, the phone
call was cut short as the money ran out.

As it got closer to 1977, I had a really bad feeling that Elvis would die.
I knew that I could not get to him, though I desperately wanted to. I
wanted to go to Graceland, but I did not have the money. I felt truly
helpless. I could feel Elvis' pain and "lostness." It was an agony that no
child should bear. Knowing that Elvis and I had a spiritual connection,
I laid in my bed and traveled to Elvis within my mind. Elvis told me
the same thing that he told me on the phone; he was alright. Even
though I knew Elvis was not alright, there was nothing more that I
could do. I hoped that, at this point, Elvis would turn his life around.
Sorrowfully, he did not. Elvis passed on into God's Kingdom."

On that day, August 16, 1977, I found himself feeling so angry with
Elvis for not changing his life. I got on my knees and shouted, "What
the heck is going on? Why do I have this strong connection? Why do I
even care?" At that moment, the path of my life took a dramatic,
different direction away from my father, Elvis. I did not want to feel
this pain I was feeling from the terrifying closeness to a man I never
even knew. It was at this point of traveling down a separate road that I
now realize when I became so very lost. Whereas, before, when my father
was alive, I was fine.

Many thoughts were running through my mind. What was going to happen to me in the future when I would need him? I did not know that Elvis had died of a heart attack and a broken heart. I thought he had died of an overdose of drugs.

This immediately made me never want to take drugs. I decided to follow Cliff Richard's clean lifestyle. I did everything I could to get away from the attachment I had with Elvis Presley. It just felt weird. I was scared of it because I did not know the reasons.

Many years had passed and it was now May 6, 2013. I had been on such a long exhausting search because I was lost inside. I did not realize that, all along, the man I was running away from for so long was the answer. I found this out first, not by DNA at all, but by giving up trying to figure out who I was and why I was so lost. I was so overwhelmingly fatigued with constantly searching to find out who I was that on this one day, I sat down and had a prayer meeting with God. I asked, "Oh God, I have been on a long journey trying to find myself. I don't know who I am and I don't think I ever will. I have always wanted to be a singer and that is what I shall be, "Elainee." Now, I will sing and make my fans, my family, and make other people happy. I will take the pain of my "lostness" and pour it into my songs. So, right now, I am making this decision to give-up and not try to find myself any longer.

Within a second, just as I was thinking about continuing my life this way, my father, Elvis Presley, appeared in my mind and he said, "This is the time that I have come to bring you home. This is who you are."

He further told me to go and sing one of his songs and then I would know. I did just that right away. I went into the next room to sing. As I walked up to the microphone, I was thinking, "This is crazy!" Then I came back to my spot on the couch. Something had happened to me which had movingly changed in my life. I had instant confidence. During all of my life, after the death of my father, I had tried so hard to gain it, but never could. I now had this wonderful sense of security and self.

It was as if I had been on a fast moving train, and now suddenly it had stopped. I was home at Graceland. All of the thousand pieces of my life kind of flew together at this magical moment. Everything instantly made sense. I knew who I was, and I knew who I looked like. Whereas before, I had no idea. My search was over now. I stood up and shouted, "Oh, my God. I'm Elvis Presley's other daughter, the real thing!" I was immediately so excited that I wanted to test my real self, so I called a bunch of my friends.

I told each of them that I had something important to tell them and that they would probably think I was completely insane. I told them that I had just figured out that I was Elvis Presley's child. None of them were surprised. They all responded, "I believe you." Later when I met up with them, they could hardly recognize me due to my new confidence. I remembers singing a song in a bar and when I got off stage, the manager said, "How come you are so much like Elvis?" I replied with, "That's because I'm Elaine Elizabeth Presley." I remember walking down the sidewalk afterwards and feeling so incredibly confident in knowing myself.

That remarkable moment of my father "bringing me home," became the moment that my road and Dad's rejoined together. I knew without a single doubt that the feeling I had for Elvis as a child was the same feeling coming into fruition. This time, I was not scared and bewildered at all. I knew that feeling was because Elvis was my father. My real father, Elvis, is inside me, and will be for the rest of my life and beyond. "I am home!"

One of the most wonderful things that I had come to recognize is that the uncomfortable feelings that I had with my other father growing up, were not family feelings like I thought they were. This was a big relief. I knew now, that the feelings I had with Elvis were what real family feelings were all about. All of the puzzle pieces finally fit together now. Finally, I understand why people truly love their families in a regular integrated way. I loved my family in just this way. I was really home.

Interestingly, at this time my sister, Lisa Marie, was living in the United Kingdom after, having moved from Los Angeles, California to start a new life. Unknowingly, Lisa was only about an hour away from me in the United Kingdom. Now, I was about to move home to Graceland to start my own new life. What a destiny in the crisscrossing of two sisters.

After my phenomenal realization, and after speaking with my friends, I strongly felt that the next step was to call Daisy and to confront her.

In the past, I had always show love to Jack and Daisy, but I never really felt it in return. I always knew that it was not normal. I asked myself, "What was wrong?" I called Daisy on the phone and told her that I had come to the conclusion about the confusion I had always felt growing up. I told Daisy that I knew what her mom wanted to tell, but never had the chance. I stated that it was not Jack who was different in the family. It was me. Also, importantly, I told her that Dennis was not my biological father. I told Daisy that Elvis Presley had been my father since his time served in Germany. Daisy reacted with, "So, you think that we are not blood relatives?" I said, "Yes, I do, and I am Elaine Elizabeth Presley." Daisy fired back with a bad attitude and said, "Well, you're never going to find out now, are you?" I replied, "I just did.

Later on, my daughter, Allison, informed me that Daisy had told her that she had not only just lost a father in death, but also a brother and sister, too. Daisy has never contacted me since. The closeness that I had tried to have with Daisy and Jack, but failed so many times during my life was no longer a worry to me. They were not my true family. I felt deep sadness. I had tried to fit in for so long in a family that was not truly mine.

I used to never mention family, but now I talk about them freely.

TO BE LOVED, TO BE HATED

In knowing my real family, I felt ecstatically free and happy. I wanted to do something big for my real family, but there was a problem. How was I going to come home to such a famous family? I could not just write a letter to Priscilla and say, "I'm your other child and am looking forward to seeing you on Wednesday!" Also, at this time, there were several other claimants trying to say that they were the lost child. Some were even trying to ridiculously claim that they were Lisa. Thus, how the heck was the real child going to make it home to Graceland?

This is where the big journey of my coming home to Graceland made its start. I knew in reality that I did not have to claim anything because I simply and truly am the real thing. I did not have to fabricate anything, create or pretend, because I was simply "me."

My grand plan was to show massive genuine love to my family by singing not only Cliff Richard's songs, but my father's as well. I set off to record two of my father's songs, "Don't Be Cruel," and "Wooden Heart." In searching out a studio, I found one just over the Welch Snowdon Mountains, just beyond the Snowdonia in England. The studio owner sounded really good on the phone, as he had recorded for some top artists, and he was a highly rated studio engineer.

But, just like everything else, nothing goes normally. The studio was supposed to be thirty-six miles away, so I decided to take this journey, on this sunny day, on my 50 CC pink retro scooter. The road I traveled on in my mind became a momentous occasion. While I was day dreaming, I missed the road around the mountain to get to the studio and ended up heading over Snowdon Mountains, which were 3,560 feet above sea level. Of course, I became very lost and cold, due to the height of the mountain. Essentially, I was riding my scooter in the clouds.

Well, five hours later, I finally arrived at my destination. It was indeed a terrifying experience. When I finally got to the right area, I could not find the studio building. After asking quite a few people, I was led to this tiny, white house with sheds and a chicken coop. It turned out that this guy was no longer operating in a big studio, but in his father's house. I ended up recording both the songs in a chicken coop. I was bent over, as the ceiling was too low. This was not a good way to sing a song. I said, "Are you sure that recording in this method is going to work?" He said, "Oh, yeah. I can fix anything. Don't worry about it."

Much later on, after releasing these two songs, even though they won awards, I knew that they were restricted and not my best work due to the cramped conditions in the "chicken coop studio." The whole thing was ridiculous and could only happen to me. On a side note, it took me under an hour to get back home traveling the right way.

The next element of my grand plan was to run the London Marathon and to support the charities that I cared about. I said to myself, "Yes, I'm going to run the London marathon on behalf of my family, Graceland, and children with cancer." I placed my entry, was accepted, and began my training. I was running and cycling forty-four miles a day, three days a week along the beautiful North Wales coastline. This became a disciplined regimen.

In the meantime, I was not happy with the records that I had released between 2011 and 2012. I was not happy with them and realized that I needed serious studio and vocal training. I enlisted the help of Jeannie Deva, an amazing celebrity vocal coach, to help me with my studio and singing issues. It turned out later that there was really not a lot wrong with my voice. I just had to learn how my voice worked so I could have the confidence to sing freely and with the correct breathing. As far as the studio, I had to be conditioned to the studio techniques. I agreed with Jeannie that I would make a CD with her vocal and studio guidance once I was back home in America. Thus, I spent considerable time in perfecting my voice, along with preparing for the London marathon.

Simultaneously, I was working on finding a manager and performing live shows. This is when I found out that I had a natural talent for the stage. People began to notice who I was. The onslaught of love and hate was pouring out heavily upon me. While the fans adored to hear me sing, other music artists were doing everything they could to bring me down. I realized how bad it was when I went to do a gig in town and another local artist threatened to close the place down if they had a Presley kid singing. They said I belonged in America, back at Graceland, and not there stealing shows from the musical locals who made their living on performing.

It became imperative for me to have a bodyguard because other artists were tracking me down and threatening violence. Even the fans were becoming so excited with my performances that I had to have a bodyguard to get out after the shows. My shows packed venues and caused a stir. It was not too much later that the live video of me singing and dancing to "Don't Be Cruel" at the Marine Hotel, Colwyn Bay, Wales on March 29, 2014 provoked an interesting phone call. They said that I was banned from moving my hips, and if I did it again, there would be severe consequences. I found out later that all of the advertising for the event had been canceled. Despite this setback, I still had the small audience "rocked" that night.

I remember being so proud in being banned for moving my hips because the same thing happened to my father back in the fifties. I have fond memories of looking up into the sky, smiling and saying, "I got banned too, Dad!" It was not over yet. One of the things I usually do after one of my shows is make a one to three song, private VIP surprise appearance, either at a charity, club, military post, or special event. On this particular night, I chose to make my special stop at a military club with about two hundred people. I sang, "Love Me Tender" with a young man in the audience on guitar. The entire audience harmonized with my singing. It was the most beautiful, heavenly sound one could ever hear.

Things escalated even more when I was starting to be verbally attacked by Elvis fans who did not want anything but Elvis. My bodyguard stopped numerous potential assaults and death threats. One of my most memorable moments was when I visited Liverpool. I had a fabulous time doing "meet and greets" for fans, as well as taking on photo opportunities, in addition to making a radio station appearance with live play. I had the thrill of visiting the Cavern, which is where the Beatles made their debut. I was overjoyed to find my photograph on the wall of the Cavern, along with other celebrities.

When this celebrity fandom event in Liverpool hit social media, the Elvis world went crazy. Instead of the world celebrating my success, Elvis fans and unknown executives closed down everything that I had achieved and made it all disappear. Here I was, just learning what my life was going to be like as the daughter of Elvis Presley. You, the reader, will continue to see, the hate against me would increase to unfathomable proportions.

I remember sitting down with my bodyguard, saying "Wow, the world has gone crazy with me coming home to Graceland."

I was also hanging out with my friends, and one of them was Betty. Betty had been diagnosed with cancer and had been suffering for quite some time. I spent a lot of time visiting her in the hospital. I had already lost quite a few friends to cancer, and it was looking like Betty might be next. She was a wonderful lady and the two of us had many great times together. Betty gave me a little "Betty Boop" compact which I cherish to this day. She was such an amazing, caring, and loving person. She owned a gravitating sense of humor, too.

And just like all of my other friends, Betty had no problem with believing the news about my father, Elvis. Betty helped me on so many levels. She was like a mother/ grandmother figure who shared her wisdom and kept me grounded. I recall Betty asking me, "Will you stay here or go back to America?" I said, "Once everything is sorted here, I will then go on home to Graceland, where I belong." I remember telling Betty that I had been lost for so long and, now, I was found and just needed to go home. Betty's health was becoming worse and she had to be rushed to the hospital. In visiting Betty in the hospital, I remember Betty asking her daughter, "Am I dying?" She passed away the next day. I was by her bedside the night before.

Two weeks later, in July, 2013, Paxton and I moved from the bungalow where we had been living and secured an apartment with security access. I continued to train for the London marathon beginning April 14th. I also continued to rehearse singing, taking keyboard lessons, and worked on new songs.

THE BIG RACE

The big day for the London marathon arrived. I was overly exuberant to be participating in this spectacular event. I was proud to be running for the crusade for kids with cancer, and also as a tribute to my father, Elvis Presley. In fact, it was like Dad and I were running side by side during the whole marathon. I took the first class train there and back because I was celebrating my "coming home to Graceland!"

A lot of people knew that I was running in this prestigious and challenging marathon. There were people there who loved and hated me. Actually, there was supposed to be a young mother with her cancer stricken daughter to meet me before the run at a "Meet and Greet," since she was such a fan of my father. In fact, I had sent her a care package of toys and dollies. I could not attend because of the avalanche of hate and attacks on me from bad Elvis fans. It was an extremely sad situation. This was horrible due to the fact that there was so much hate involved in a place where I had planned to provide support for a cancer patient. This situation made me realize what my life was going to be like as a child of Elvis Presley.

Behind the scenes, before the marathon started, things were wonderful. I had the opportunity to endorse other charities, such as the Samaritans, and I had my photograph taken alongside top runners. I knew that both my fans and enemies had turned up for this event. Throughout this marathon, I felt as if I was running home to Graceland.

The big race started and the celebration began. People shouted and cheered me on along the way. The smiling, joyous faces were amazing. I quickly realized that I had to keep my eye out for enemies. An enemy appeared on the sidelines. It was a man that had an evil look and glared at me. I glared back at him and he backed off. He was probably one of the haters that was attacking my cancer patient. I gave him the Presley look that meant, "don't mess with me."

I passed him, and all of the celebrating faces and shouts continued. It was not too long later, while on a trail during the run, water was being offered to me every step of the way. I was suspiciously offered water from one of the other runners. I noticed that it was in a different kind of bottle, so I declined it.

Finally, just over six hours later, I came to the end of the race. It was an awesome feeling, to say the least, to flash through that fabulous finish line. I said, "Dad, we did it, and for such a wonderful cause!" Everyone was proud of me, and I was proud of myself, too. After my massage and friendship talk, people said to me, "What are you going to do now?" I immediately stated that I was going home to Graceland.

A funny thing happened when I was sitting in the first class lounge waiting for the train. A man approached me and said, "Elaine Presley?" I responded with, "Yes, Sir?" He then said, "I only have one thing to say to you." I replied back, in exhilaration, "It was so fantastic running the marathon for my Dad and for kids with cancer!" He kind of choked up. I felt that he might have been about to tell me something really evil, but he could not after seeing how happy I was.. He, right then, and there, shook my hand and stormed out of the lounge as fast as he could. I shouted out to him in progress saying, "Sir, what was it you wanted to say to me?", but he was gone.

There was a couple sitting opposite of me and they were smiling in my direction. The man said, "How are you doing, Elaine?" I was shocked that he knew my name. He immediately ordered the staff to come over to me. He gave them some hand signals, and the lady staff member said to me, surprising me, "Would you like to get a shower and get into your jammies for bedtime?" He mentioned that it was nice to meet me and knew that I must be tired. It was time for me to go to bed. I went on and had a shower, got into the pajamas provided me, and then went to sleep in the first class lounge. To this day, I do not know who that man was that was so kind to me on that train.

BACK AND ONWARD

It was a happy trip back home. I held tight to the memory of running to daddy and treasuring my medallion, all while helping kids with cancer. I was thinking that this was the best way to make my homecoming at Graceland, by just being myself. Also, I was thinking, "Well, it should be fine for me to go home now and to be accepted by my family." At this time, in my naive state, I was the happiest girl in the whole world. I had no idea just how hard it was getting ready to rain on my parade.

Also, during this time, I received a phone call from Irene. She had come to the conclusion that we needed to dissolve our prior music contract, but wanted to remain friends.

Thankfully, this "musical breakup" proved to be best for both of us. It was a test of the strength and credibility of our friendship. As individuals, we truly respected each other's talents and music careers.

In October, 2014, I began planning on appearing on the "Rew and Who" program in New York City; October 15th and 17th. The day after the last show, I rented a car and traveled to Virginia to venture back to the home where I had lived when I first came over to America in 1984. While standing outside the house, I cried my eyes out. I really treasured that simple time. I remembered all of the family love in that home.

There were so many wonderful memories. Now, that time was gone. I was standing in the past.

After going on to a few other places in memorabilia, I stayed in a hotel in Williamsburg, Virginia. It was gratifying to experience having numerous people come up to me with warm greetings and asking for my autograph.

On the way back to New York City, I remember thinking, "I need to return to England and close out everything, and then go to Graceland as soon as possible." I could not just remain in America and head home to Graceland at that point. I still had obligations back in England to Paxton. I also needed to finalize all of my accounts and records. Thus, due to these circumstances, my journey home to Graceland had to be delayed. I hesitantly returned back to England.

Venturing back and forth from the United Kingdom to America did not present itself as a real big problem at this time. This visit to the United Kingdom was just going to be for two weeks. Nevertheless, I did have some immigration obstacles because I had been out of the United States and living in England for too long. First, my paperwork was out of order. I was arrested at Kennedy airport as I was going through Immigration. They asked me why my papers were out of date, and why I had she been out of the country for such a long time. I explained that I had been ill and that I had also been taking care of other people who had fallen ill. I informed them that I only needed to be in the states this time for two weeks to conclude my business matters before returning to the United Kingdom. I made it clear that as soon as possible, I would be returning to the United States on a lasting basis. With that, the homeland security officials issued me a deportation order with my hearing a year later. In light of this experience, I felt that I was lucky to be allowed to re-enter the United States without being thrown in jail. I knew that upon my next permanent return, I would be facing much more serious immigration issues.

I landed in the United Kingdom and went home to Paxton. I gave him a thorough explanation of why I had to return to America. I proceeded to shut-down all of my important personal business. In doing so, I closed my bank accounts and two real estate companies. I then transferred my car and all of my other possessions that I owned in the United Kingdom to Paxton. I gave Paxton the offer to come with me, but he was pure English/Welsh and had no intentions of ever leaving England. Paxton understood the reasoning behind my decision to return to America. He knew that I had to continue my journey, realization my destiny, and to be back with my daughter and family.

Originally, when I moved back to England, it was supposed to be a short visit of about six months, but I accidentally created a little life there for myself.

In the ensuing months, I found myself in a major business dilemma. I had been a top real estate business consultant with a 98% success rate. One of the biggest things that I advised my clients to never do was get to involve investors, unless they could afford to lose the money. Many investors like to play the ego game and think that they are being creative. Going against my natural knowledge of this, and since I was feeling a lull as far as real estate activity and wanting to have a change, I took on some investors who claimed that they were wealthy. One group even signed paperwork that claimed they had at least 500,000 pounds in liquid cash.

The big bold plan was for this association of people to give me 10% of what I needed, with a balance due to me later. I did not know that they borrowed the money from multiple family members. In doing this, the scheme made it look legitimate. But when it came time for them to pay the bulk of the cash, they simply did not have it. They tried to bully me into creating the rest of the money for them. I realized this was an enormous scam of theirs to get rich off of my ingenuity. Instead of legally keeping their 10%, I paid that money back to their parents who could not afford to lose it. Afterwards, I executed a hostile corporate takeover and closed-out the companies involved, making them debt free.

The last part of my regimen to close down my existence in England was to have a full physical. I had postponed this physical for too long, out of fear. It became even more serious to address my health since I had been feeling generally unwell. I only had two months left to return to America for my hearing session, and this was something that I definitely could not miss. The consequences for not returning would have been horrible.

When I went to get the results of my tests, the doctor asked me, "What are your plans?" I responded, "To return to America as soon as I can." The doctor replied, "Based on your medical test results, I'm scared for you to even leave the office." My doctor then stated that she might need to hospitalize me. I tried to convince the doctor that these negative results just attributed to me being under horrific stress because of all the people who had recently died. The doctor then agreed that if I took newly prescribed medications and underwent multiple xrays and scans, that she would allow me to leave. I could tell by the look on the doctor's face that she didn't think I could make it to the parking lot. I was very surprised that she did not hospitalize me.

I left the office and went on to pick up my new medicine. On the way to the pharmacy, I was so terrified that I thought I would have a nervous breakdown. In conclusion of this doctor visit and subsequent hospital tests, it became evident that I was dealing with hereditary medical issues similar to my father. In fact, I was close to the same situation as my father was back in 1977.

Yet, all I had on my mind was to get back to my daughter, Allison, and to Graceland. At this time, I did not believe that I had much more time to live. I was about to make one of the stupidest decisions of my life, but I chose to move ahead. My thoughts were misguiding me to stop taking these new prescriptions and to get a second opinion in America. The whole purpose behind the madness was to get on that plane and pretend that I was not ill. To this day, it is indeed a miracle that I survived.

Paxton took me to the airport and I got on that plane. This was one of the hardest emotional moments of my life, leaving Paxton and Quaver. Because of my medical condition, I did not know if I would ever see them all again. I had no other choice but to do this, as my daughter and family were in America. It was not my fault that Paxton did not want to come. I thought to myself, "I have no idea how I will survive, as I only have seven hundred dollars in my purse. I am very sick and not nearly as young as I used to be. I will have to be functioning on the streets in New York City." I estimated my survival rate at about one percent. That was not in consideration of everything. I was about to face immigration.

Without my knowledge, on top of all the odds against me, there were my father's fans calling the authorities. These fans were trying to convince the officials that a fake and criminal daughter of Elvis Presley, who is really a man, was about to enter the country.

OUT OF THE GATE, IN HIGH WATER

The plane landed in New York City and my mind and body quickly went into survival mode. I was certain that I was going straight to jail due to my immigration issues. This gave me a false sense of comfort in thinking that I would have a place to sleep and food to eat.

I went through immigration and was immediately detained by the authorities. In the midst of the shock, I felt an overwhelming sense of total peace because I knew who I was. Only a real child of Elvis Presley would say what I was about to say next. The department of homeland security took my fingerprints and I went through extensive interrogations for many hours. One of the first questions they asked me was, "Who is your father?" I sat up in the chair and said without reservation, "My father is Elvis Presley, Sir."

After this sequence, I felt that I would definitely be headed for the "dungeon." Surprisingly, the immigration officer said that this was not the father that I had listed on my application from 1984. I then stated, "I know, Sir. I only found this out in 2013." He asked me why I was gone for so long and I explained that I had been very sick and how I had to look after not only myself, but many other people who were ill. I told him that I did not mean to be gone for so long. I further explained that I just wanted to come back home to Graceland and to my daughter.

He then proceeded to ask me about my gender issues. He took a great deal of notes. After the questioning, I was told to sit in a chair and wait while the officer disappeared for quite awhile. At this point, I was afraid that I might not be let into the country. In my heart, I knew that I must be allowed to enter. I was totally transparent regarding the facts of my life and I openly disclosed the identity of my real father.

Everybody in the room looked so strict and scary to me. I knew they had the power to send me away. The original officer finally reappeared and signaled for me to come to his desk. He stated that he could easily put me in a temporary jail there at the airport. I replied, "Yes, I know that, Sir, but I just want to go home." He told me to go back and sit in my seat and that he would be back in a minute. He left me again for approximately thirty minutes and then returned to talk to the guard and other staff members. The guard walked over to me and asked if I needed any water and whether or not I was hungry. The guard also me if I would like to use his cell phone to call anyone. I politely declined, "No, thank you."

The officer then called me over to his desk again. He stamped a few papers and then looked up at me and said, "You know that you have an immigration hearing coming up?" I said, "Yes, Sir, I do." He then stood up and said, "Welcome home, Ms. Presley. The exit is over there." I innately knew that somebody important must have been speaking to them. It seemed it went from a completely tough army environment to big giant smiling faces with halos above their heads. Their eyes followed me straight out to the exit.

Getting out of airport security was an enormous relief to me. I knew then that I had truly made it. I was thankfully aware that I was on my way home to my friends and family.

This next part was an extremely emotional time for me. Suddenly, reality hit me and I realized that I was just outside of security at the airport with two big pieces of luggage, passing everybody who was being hugged and greeted by their loving families. I was actually looking around for Lisa and Priscilla, which was crazy because I knew that they could not be, just like my own daughter. I did not have the love and support that I had when I first had when I came over from the United Kingdom to the United States in 1984. I realized at that moment that I was alone with my two bags and only seven hundred dollars in my pocket. I was terrified.

The first thing I did was take the train into New York City. By this time, one of my bags had broken. I was forced to buy another one. This unavoidable purchase left me with $650.00. I faced the fact that I had to secure these bags quickly, as they were just too heavy to carry around. I went to a public computer to research my options. I decided my best choice was to secure a very small storage unit in Manhattan. I thought that if I were to be homeless, I might as well be homeless on 5th Avenue in Manhattan. After all, the cheapest apartment would be around $5,000 per month, and I was living there on the streets for free.

I found a small hostel that I was able to move into right away. It was certainly not like the old days when one could live in a spot like this for almost free. This hostel was $110.00 a night in a room with eight beds. I had one of the bottom bunks at the back. For the most part, everyone staying there were students and they had nightly entertainment. I had a blast with the students at the comedy shows. For a short time, everything in my life seemed almost normal.

Two days later, however, I had to move out. The next place I found was in the Bronx. It was a tiny, poverty-stricken motel in the center of gang territory. The persons that ran this motel were pretty dodgy. In fact, I discovered that most people who booked rooms in this motel were from Russia and other countries. It seemed their stays were short, all wanting to get out of there as soon as their weekly payment ran out. They all stayed in bunk beds and had to scramble to find sheets. I managed to stay in the motel for three days and then I quickly checked-out.. I did feel fortunate, though, as there was one Russian gentleman who had to return to his country facing persecution.

There I found myself, again on the streets of Manhattan with only fifty dollars to my name. As the night started to fall, I began to panic, standing in the darkness with sobbing eyes. I did not want to, but I felt I had no choice. I asked a stranger where I could find a homeless shelter and for the directions on how to get there. In having no experience with this, I had no idea that there were separate shelters; one for women and one for men. The directions I was given led me to the mens' homeless shelter.

I stood at the front desk in tears telling them I was homeless and had nowhere to go. This normally would have been a very bad thing to do because the people there were experienced homeless people. The front desk clerk looked at a fellow employee and said, "This girl has turned up here. Go and get the manager!" The manager, who was female, came down the stairs and asked me to follow her upstairs with her. She apologized and said that it was too late to admit anyone in that they were closed. There was nothing she could do for me in that moment. She politely asked me my name and I told her, "Elaine Elizabeth Presley." She replied, "Wait here!"

When she came back, she sat down and gave me some travel cards, money, and told me that one of their security guards was going to escort me to a church where I could stay for the night. We had to walk about two miles. While we walked, we talked along the way and the kindly officer said to me, "Now, you can begin thinking about yourself, your life, and how you can help others." I stopped him right away and told him that I had always helped other people. He smiled at me and told me how he thought that that was a very good thing.

A RAINBOW WAITING

The church where I stayed provided me with a chair for me to sleep in, which was looked after by two security guards. The next morning I was sent to a womens' shelter in Manhattan. Upon arriving, they said that I could stay there as long as I needed. I soon discovered that I loved it there and that I fit right in. I lived in a dorm with about forty other women. We spent a lot of time talking. We even went to church on a regular basis. We also enjoyed going out for coffee and spent quality time together sharing our stories and experiences.

There was one black woman there who was seventy-eight years old who had been living there for twenty years. Keep in mind that this was a homeless dwelling, and this woman had been homeless for that amount of time. I became immediately disgusted that not one business person in New York had taken it upon themselves to put this deprived lady in her own habitat. This proved to be a particular time in which I wished I still had lots of money. There was no question that I would have found her a home of her own.

The staff treated me very well and made me feel special, often giving me gifts. It was actually a very structured place, but full of love. I was living in the heart of Manhattan with many friends I had made. There was the harsh reality, however, that this place was also incredibly dangerous with residents who were ex-prisoners, drug addicts, and persons with extreme mental issues. Contracting a disease would be very easy since there were so many sick people living there. I could feel the impending dangers lurking every single day.

I had actually been only staying there about two weeks when a lady approached me with a nice big grin and asked, "How would you like the opportunity to live in a luxury house with full sponsorship for eighteen months to get your life in order?" She went on to say that they would give me full assistance and funding until I could get my life together and find employment, for which they would help me. They also stated that there would be conditions and rules to follow. In the first six months of residency, it was mandatory that I rest.

In awe, I went to see the house and it was totally amazing, not to mention completely secure. The total sponsorship package that I was offered equaled to approximately two million dollars. I agreed, but expressed that ultimately I wanted to get home to Graceland. In accordance, they made it clear that I first had to get my life straight there. At this phase, I had not spent one night on the streets. There was one technicality.

When I first landed in New York City, I was supposed to go and visit a friend in St. Louis, Missouri. That friend was Irene Leland. I was too embarrassed to call and tell her that I was almost out of money. I never had any inclination to call anybody, especially a friend, and put myself on their doorstep. I was in an awkward position. The good news was that after my being in New York City for two weeks, I had a sense of feeling secure knowing that I had a very good place to go. Through subsequent phone conversations with Irene, she made it clear that I was welcomed and insisted that I come to stay with her in St. Louis. I kept telling Irene over and over that I did not want to be a burden on a friend.

Upon analyzing these two very enticing offers, I made the craziest decision of my life. I gave-up all of the safety and my financial security of staying in Manhattan with that wonderful offer. I chose to leave that behind and go to St. Louis for two reasons. First, I did not desire to break my promise to Irene. Secondly, that spot in St. Louis was closer to Memphis, Tennessee. I was given money by the homeless shelter to take the coach to St. Louis.

It was a two-day jaunt to St. Louis. I could not help thinking that my long original journey home to Memphis, Tennessee, was about to become realized. St Louis was just 250 miles away from my home. I took the long and tedious bus ride to St. Louis, calling Irene to let her know that I was on my way. I arrived on October 7, 2015. I could not help but think, "Oh, my. I've just put my whole life on the line!" I called Irene on what little battery power that I had left on my free New York city phone and said, "Hi! I'm here." Irene was relieved and very happy to know that I had made it safely to St Louis.

Meeting Irene brought forward a distinct combination of both joy and fear for me. No question, I was overjoyed to see her, but on the other hand, I was placing all of my faith in the hands of Irene. In clarification, I had always had control of my life before this big move, and now I had relinquished that control to somebody else, something that I had never done before. Nevertheless, there I was embarking on a major new advancement. I went from total survival mode to putting my trust into someone else.

A NEW THRESHOLD IN LIFE

Irene picked me up from the bus stop in downtown St. Louis. We drove back to Irene's home in Brentwood, Missouri. At this point, we had no idea what adventures would lie ahead.

Irene lived in a two-story brick colonial house. It appeared to be a cozy little house from the front view, but as the car made its way up the drive, the house seemed to grow into another house in the back. The previous owners had an addition built on the back-end of the structure, including a brick patio from the early seventies. The original house dates back to 1964. Irene had spent almost forty years of her life in this home which was filled with many wonderful memories.

My first reaction, as Irene took me on a brief initial tour inside the home, was "Oh, it feels so very English!" This pleased Irene, as it was nice to know that the interior accents and "feel" of the house responded automatically well with my familiarity. Irene's heritage was definitely English. I had a natural concept and knowledge of that. The home retained and exuded an interesting mixture of distinctive and impressive antiques; English, French, and Victorian, combined with bits of Colonial and Ranch elements.

Irene's maternal grandfather, Robert Leathan Lund's mother, Sarah Stephenson, is the niece of the "Grandfather of the Railroad", George

Stephenson, the inventor of the steam engine and the builder of the first railroad between Manchester and Liverpool, England in 1835.

Irene had a family room, which was part of the addition to the back of the house. It was strikingly similar to the "Jungle Room" of Graceland; from the wood walls, wood ceiling beams, the same type of carpeting, and even a duplicate of a lamp shade.

Irene had been cheerily preparing for my visit and it made her happy that her now recently renovated two upstairs rooms would be occupied. I found a comfortable, cozy spot in the guest room and, soon after, an office/private work space in the newly created "fun room", as Irene called it. It was a happy room filled with all kinds of collections with everything from foreign dolls, penguin figurines, and teddy bears. I settled-in and got the hang of things.

Irene's home life conveyed every bit of "down home", easy-going, self-proclaimed nature. As the days moved onward, I keenly picked up on the overall ambiance and attitude that surrounded Irene's old world. I am so much like my father; very simple country folk. One of the biggest worries in my mind regarding eventually coming home to Graceland was whether I would be able to fit-in with Lisa, Priscilla, and the rest of the family in their high celebrity life style.

SETTING THE PACE

Irene and I kept authenticating and shoring up our friendship. We utilized our individual assets and helped each other. I had a lot of technical and computer knowledge, which helped Irene immensely. She was consistently introducing me to her friends, her family, and individuals within her community.

Irene and I both had a bolstering affinity for music. I worked on putting Irene in touch with good contacts and sources and I gave her original songs to get her more exposure. Irene admired my musical talent as a singer, songwriter, and performer..

While staying at Irene's home, my help to her and the family was unwavering. Also, I took on a huge brunt of the chores of the house, inside and out, not to mention running errands and shopping for household needs. While I was extremely helpful to Irene, I was also very grateful for her hospitality.

Even though I had to continually face the challenges of being the daughter of the King, I forged through it all. I put all of my energy into organizing and establishing a working plan for myself, in not only utilizing my past professional experiences, but also in reaching out in research for new avenues to navigate. I found employment as an investigator for federal and private agencies. I demonstrated well my persevering and tenacious abilities in this realm. I diligently and devotedly poured out my avid efforts in creating my own publishing company, L&L Presley LLC. Also, my charity causes were always a priority through the Elaine Elizabeth Presley Foundation.

Irene soaked up the joy of introducing me to her many friends, as well as family members. It could not have been more thrilling and satisfying to encounter the pleasing reactions from each of these dear persons in Irene's life. Over and over, they were all totally enchanted with me. They appreciated my outgoing, sincere effervescence, endearing English accent, and witty British humor. All of these people made me feel like a "shining star" within a family of friends.

In settling into my new St. Louis environment and way of life, one of the major things that I had to address was my health. I had obviously been procrastinating on this important issue for a long time. But, just like my father who had spiritually been there for me ever since I was born, he was here for me again at this time, too. He showed himself in many ways, especially at this moment when I needed help and assistance.

I was on the computer and a video from Larry Geller, my father's hairdresser and spiritual adviser, popped up. He was speaking about how Elvis took too long to get help as far as the health condition that he and I both share together. I immediately woke up from viewing this, knowing that it was part of the road map that my father had left me to follow. Next, I did two things. First, I booked an appointment with a doctor, and then I contacted Larry Geller to thank him for the informative video. In this process, we talked about not only how this was a "meant to be," but I thanked him for saving my life. He was most gracious. I will always consider Larry a good friend and someone whom I can trust.

In Irene's basement, there was an old radio, circa 1960, that I discovered. Even though Irene said that it should be discarded, I felt an urge to hold onto it. In pulling it out of the "rubble," I accidentally dropped it on the hard, cement basement floor. Irene proclaimed, "Don't worry about it. It's now history, just throw it away!" Despite this, I felt a compelling feeling of closeness and brought the supposed "dead" radio back upstairs and placed it in the upstairs study. As soon as I plugged it in and turned it on, not knowing what station it had been left on, "Are You Lonesome Tonight," by Elvis, played promptly.

Now that I had taken care of my health issues, I realized again how lucky I was to be alive. I vowed to always take care of myself medically. Now that this issue had been taken care of, I had other major things to be concerned about such as money and homeland security. It turned out that the costs for homeland security and immigration needs were going to be tremendous and would involve approximately about a three year legal battle. I found one of the top lawyers, which was a good thing to get used to because my life had become ruled by lawyers, confidants and managers, since I was the daughter of Elvis Presley.

When I first "came home," I did everything I could to entertain the public because I loved making the fans happy. Soon, I understood that the unauthorized and unorganized public appearances were to stop without clearance. So, there I sat, living in the "behind the scenes" life, feeling beaten down by all of the punishment. I finally got my act together and did things correctly through my team. Doing things professionally is a must for me. All of my legal problems were taken care of at the initial cost of 1.2 million dollars.

All of the lawyers who represented me were superior attorneys in their respective fields, and my personal business lawyer previously worked on cases related to my father. As well as my legal team, I also feel I have the best medical team.

I am ever so proud to be home at Graceland, running my company and foundation from Graceland. Both my company and foundation are debt free. Although my company is newly formed, it has maintained a five star reputation in Memphis, Tennessee.

Originally, before I "came home," my desire was to form Boden House for the homeless. Then later, when I came home, it would become "Presley House." I discovered that my sister, Lisa Marie, had already formed "Presley Place." Thus, I established the "Elaine Elizabeth Presley Wish Foundation."

HOMEWARD TO GRACELAND

I was in wonder and magical expectation of taking the long anticipated trip to my "homeland," Graceland. I experienced the glory and fulfillment of this marvel on two holiday visits, a year apart, while living with Irene. The initial "entrance" encompassed a two day visit right before Christmas in 2016. To say the least, it was an extraordinary phenomenon to be greeted so warmly and highly by all of the great folks at Graceland, and to be so graciously treated by everyone. The enchantment of encountering my father's beautiful grave on the site at Graceland was the most affecting and stirring involvement ever.

Upon my first time being at "home" after 56 years, I found myself very emotional while making it up the driveway to be by the side of my father. I was administered a wonderful surprise by being able to help decorate my father's grave for Christmas with beautiful flowers and roses. I have had many spiritual happenings with my father. For example, it was raining during my first visit to Graceland and I could not get my umbrella to stay up. I felt that my father was saying, "Let the world see you on camera by my side." After praying at my father's side, I left before the visitors arrived. As I walked down to the gate, my umbrella opened up by itself, working perfectly again. I smiled, looked up, and said, "Thank you, Dad!"

Before I came back to St. Louis, I had the thrill of going down to my father's house in Mississippi. I entertained the fans there, showing them around, and swinging on the swing like I used to do as a kid in the United Kingdom. One of the fans said, "We know you are family because you look like Elvis sitting there."

The following excursion to Graceland happened in 2017 for a three day venture, revolving around Christmas. It was another tremendously enjoyable and satisfying time. What made this trip very special was that I was put in contact with Elvis's best friend from early childhood, Leroy. It was a thrill beyond measure to go to his home in Arkansas and to meet him and his son, Michael. Of course, the memories abounded, and what a profound pleasure it was for me to hear all of the great stories. I held the classic original guitar that Leroy and Elvis had bought together with every penny that they could jointly scratch up.

TRAVELING TO SING

Two very stimulating, out-of-town musical events were on their way to unfolding. In August, 2017, Irene and I were invited to attend the X-Poze-Ing Music Awards show at the Madison Street Theater in Chicago. We were both honored with the request to perform. I had already been declared the mascot of the ceremony and Irene was pleased to have previously won their "Best Song" awards in her categories. It was exhilarating beyond belief for the accolades that Irene and I both received at the end of the show. What a celebration. I was bestowed the "Outstanding Musician" award, and Irene garnered two top awards for the year for both "Folk" and "Singer/Songwriter."

I was very excited to be part of, and also to represent my family, at a big extravaganza for saving the animals of the world; "World Peace for Animals" at the Isis music hall in Asheville, North Carolina in November, 2017. I got a huge bang out of being on stage for this event with famous "Hall of Fame" artists and bands. When I gave my spiel, I proclaimed to the audience, "Don't be cruel to the animals." Then, I launched into singing, "Don't Be Cruel."

THE UTMOST GIFTS

Irene and I were astounded and overtaken with gratification when we were notified in 2017 that we each were receiving customized, painted guitars, made for us by the renowned artist and minister, Austin Turner in Memphis. This was indeed a high honor. We were informed that Turner considers these works of art not gifts from him, but gifts from God.

We were so ecstatic upon receiving our guitars that we took videos of each other opening up these gems; step by step, hand by hand, until the treasures burst out of the box. They looked amazing. Each one was so perfectly crafted, not only in artistry, but in personalized execution, designed with the rich identity of the owner while portraying individualized theme through style, color, and natural character.

Irene and I learned that we were also about to receive "icing on the cake." Austin Turner was in the process of creating his highly regarded "Austibirds" for Irene and me. These exquisite birds are gloriously handcrafted in fine detail with each proud recipient in mind. Each "Bird" could not have been more gorgeous. It was a fulfilling effort to hang each one of these treasures on the wall.

SYNCHRONICITY ABOUNDS

Call it serendipity, synchronicity, or simply fate, but there has been a whole surreal amount of it uncannily and meaningfully happening to me. Whether it presents itself as little or big stuff, each realization and/or occurrence is poignant and brings it all together for me.

In the summer of 2016, I went to the exciting musical performance of "All Shook Up" at the famous St. Louis Municipal Opera. It was a revival of Elvis's greatest hits incorporated into a zany and captivating plot. There were so many unbelievable moments in the production which chimed in alignment with my life that it literally gave me goosebumps. One moment in particular was the name of the amusement park in the small fictional town where big scenes were played on one of the main stage sets. The name was featured on a huge backdrop sign. It was called, "Funland." That strikingly caught my eyes as it was the same as the amusement park in Great Yarmouth in England where I had worked during the summer at the age of thirteen.

I was elated to meet a lovely lady named Bobbi in early 2017. It was a beautiful "afternoon visit" which lasted eight hours. I was mesmerized by all of the Elvis memorabilia that Bobbi brought with her. There were letters, postcards, 45 records, pictures with Elvis from visits to Graceland, and an Elvis signed movie poster which was still in a frame.

The most highly emotional moment was when Bobbi presented me with a darling, small vintage frame, holding the original dried roses from Elvis's grave that her mom had brought home with her after going down to the funeral. Bobbi had saved these treasured rose petals and had placed them in the customized frame for me. I was overtaken by this lovely surprise. Just two weeks prior, I was praying to my father and asking him for a small memento from him.

The meeting with Bobbi was special. It meant so much to me and our meeting came at a time when I was feeling the brunt of the "haters" and disbelievers all around. In sadness, Bobbi only lived another few months. I am eternally grateful to have gotten to know her, even for that brief, but meaningful time.

In March 2017, I had the supreme joy of attending the truly magnificent musical performance of "Million Dollar Quartet" at the St. Louis Repertory Theater. Of course, Elvis was one of the main characters and, to put it mildly, this show brought the house down a million times over. There energy felt during the show effectively carried me away in happiness.

On April 9, 2017, I was overwhelmingly grateful to be able to attend a celebratory funeral; a four and a half hour service at the Pageant in St. Louis, honoring the life of the legendary original King of Rock and Roll, Chuck Berry. There were so many amazing testimonials. One outstanding testimonial was given by a famous singer who talked about a vivid memory of when Elvis walked into an establishment where Berry was performing and pointed out to him on stage, "That is the real King of rock 'n' roll!" I desired to go to this important event on behalf of my father and family. This was an occasion that my father would not wish to miss; celebrating the life of the original king of rock 'n' roll.

Another profound moment in my life came early one morning when I came downstairs and was confronted with a perfect image of Elvis's face illuminated in Irene's family room window. It manifested from the brake lights of Irene's car, which malfunctioned and turned on. It created a bright three dimensional effect of the image that illuminated the entire family room. I knew it was my father. I was mesmerized with a feeling of protection and peace from my father. To this day, the image of Elvis remains in Irene's window.

Irene was so excited to introduce me to Victoria Price, the daughter of Vincent Price. It all happened when Victoria came to St. Louis in March, 2018 to give a talk and book signing regarding her new book, "The Way of Being Lost." What an overwhelming jubilation it was for me, the daughter of the King of Rock and Roll to meet the daughter of the King of Horror. Victoria and I had a blast, to say the very least. Irene's mother, Dorothy, had a long romance with Vincent culminating in their engagement in 1935. Dorothy had to break the engagement due to family matters, but they stayed close friends until their deaths, only 16 days apart, in 1993. I wholeheartedly expressed to Victoria, "It's so very special to meet you, as I feel close to you and your father while staying at Irene's. I have said since I came to visit Irene that I was saved by the King of Horror for the King of Rock 'n' Roll!" Victoria and I had our photo taken together.

During Victoria's talk, she spoke often about her history of feeling "lost," which of course rang a humongous bell with me. I felt "lost" for so long, just as Victoria, yet in totally different ways. What struck a big note was that Victoria shared about her finding her truest self by letting go of all of the pressures put upon her and just tuning into her heart and being herself. This is exactly what I was doing, too. Victoria summed everything up with the importance of feeling "joy" every single day.

As Irene and I were driving away from this moving and inspiring discussion, I broke into the verbal exhilaration of how I tremendously felt that this recent experience was "meant to be."

A beautiful, maternal moment was when I took red roses with small diamonds in them to my Mother, Priscilla Presley, in December 2014. She had a lead role in Snow White and The Seven Dwarfs, at The Opera House in Manchester, England.

One of the biggest changes my life was when I was exclusively invited to attend the private premier of Elvis Presley's "The Searcher" documentary with Priscilla Presley, the woman I know to be my mother. This highly earmarked, early movie showing and cocktail reception was held at the Belcourt Theater and Cabana's in the heart of Nashville, Tennessee on March 18, 2018.

The documentary unveiled many key and driving actualities, and in its unexampled way, subtly endorsed my life. I was not surprised that I felt even more close to Priscilla seeing her in person. It was almost like Dad was reaching out in spirit to bring everyone together. The film itself was as if it was also telling the story of myself, as well as father. From the bike scene in the beginning with the playing cards and pegs in the wheels, to the fascinating "road map," searching for who we both were.

A third memorable moment in my life was when I had dinner with my Mother, at the Hilton Hotel in Memphis, Tennessee. She received a Distinguished Citizen award June 24th, 2018, and her acceptance speech was one of the proudest moments of my life.

Factually, Dad and I, unbeknownst to each other, visited black churches, and there has been a lot of incorrect information about why we did this. The truth is that white churches did not give either of us the musical, soulful feel that we needed. Black people did not teach Dad or me how to move our legs and hips. This was already natural for us to do. Black churches gave us both the spiritual vehicle that we needed to bring out and release our deep, soulful feelings that we both had inside of us.

Dad became lost after the death of his mother. I became lost after the death of my father. Dad found himself intensely searching all of his life, trying to find the answer to the purpose of his existence. When his career took him down many dark roads, he became even more lost. But, by going through this painful process, he found that what he was searching for was already inside his own heart, and that was God and family, which is the real Foundation. In his "seeking" journey, Dad created a natural "road map," which he passed onto his family. Dad's destiny was to entertain his fans, and that was what he did to the highest degree. The road map Dad naturally created was a mighty gift and privilege for Lisa and me.

I also received another great gift on the day of the documentary viewing, and it was a gift from Priscilla Presley. Priscilla's inspirational words of creating projects and meaningful missions opened up my eyes. I was really feeling "Home" now.

The Big Deal

About four years after I "came home", I was approached by a confidante and associate of my Dad's to create an offer for me to hand to the executives of Authentic Brands, which purchased the rights to Elvis Presley. The offer comprised of five million in cash and approximately twenty million in rights, assets, and privileges. There was, however, one catch. The confidante wanted to change my voice on any recordings, and the way that I represented myself as a person.

Since I had been lost and had no confidence before I came home to my family, and then became totally found on May 6, 2013, there was no way and no amount of money in the world that would ever get me to change who I am. No way. It is natural.

I declined the offer, stating that I wanted to stay being true to myself.

This made the confidant upset, since he had spent weeks on trying to re-train me into the way that he desired me to be. He was able to get past it and, happily, the confidant and I are still friends.

Later, I realized that some of the things that the confidant wanted to do made sense to my survival within a big corporate world. Those with the power controlled everything, in the same way that they did with my father. So far, I have been able to remain being myself, but at a very costly price.

My father summed it up in one of his quotes: "The image is one thing, and the human being is another." This lesson is part of the road map that Elvis Presley left our family to maintain; 'being yourself." Within that, to be great and never allow anybody to change you into a false persona that you cannot continue to live up to.

DNA EXPOSED

When I first realized who I truly was and shouted it to the world, the world reacted with, "Okay, show us your DNA test and then we will believe you." It was not as easy as that, because when I did take my DNA test, the world responded with, "No, no, no, it's fake DNA!" Also, it did not help that Elvis's body guards were still trying to protect him, in saying that anybody claiming to have his DNA was false. In all honesty, and in anybody's rational mind, how would any of these security people even know? It is only rumors. Then, there are executives, fans, and media trying to protect father, as well. I appreciate all of these people, and also believe that most of the claims seeking money are indeed fake. However, this protection really hurts a real child trying to go home.

We all know that the media does not make money off of positive stories. If I had been fake, investigative reporters would have had a field day by now. I have been investigated by a lot of them. It needs to be remembered that I have given up my life to come home to my family at Graceland and in continuing the legacy. It upsets me that the outside claimants have no real desire to "come home" and continue their supposed father's legacy. I have personally stopped millions of dollars in fake claims in my attempts to protect my father's legacy and pocketbook.

However, when you are the real child of Elvis Presley, it is extremely painful and frustrating when you have to fight every inch of your way to be home at Graceland, desperately wanting to continue my legacy and to build Graceland. I want to utilize the gifts God gave me and to share my life experiences. In all that time of being held back by ignorant people who fail to correctly see who I really am, I did not "come home" to gain money. I have a tremendous amount of business skills, many of which Graceland has already taken advantage of. I would be a success without being the child of Elvis Presley. The only reason I came home was because Graceland is my home and I am devotedly fighting to be able to do my job that is within my rightful legacy. How does a real, legitimate child of Elvis Presley do her dutiful job when the world is filled with so much ridiculousness and insanity?

Well, the first answer is to solve this question of DNA. I have been completely honest, open, and transparent since the day I realized who I was. Additionally, this book is a complete and accurate document of my entire life. I clearly desire to convey to anyone out there, "You can totally know me really well. There has never been anything hidden. There are no excuses. There are no reasons why I cannot show you something. This book is the whole truth and nothing but the truth, so help me God!"

So, let's get down to the cold, hard DNA investigative facts. As far as myself, having experience as an investigator, I will now display the facts. My very first investigation was by the British government. No one ever said that I was not who I really am. My second investigation was by

Homeland Security and the FBI. It needs to be explained that this was an extreme investigation, including intense interrogation and inspection of my entire life; blood tests, fingerprints, and a mental/physical examination. In results of this extensive four year criterion, I was evaluated and confirmed to be Elaine Elizabeth Presley, daughter of Elvis Presley, and my paperwork shows this.

Even though the government has my father listed as Elvis Presley and recognizes me as such, the federal government cannot endorse "out of Wedlock" children. It is the United States federal law.

The next investigation was done by a private security company in France. In taking my DNA from my fingerprints, they kept most of the testing secret, yet they sent me a quick message saying that I definitely was the child of Elvis Presley.

The next validating evidence came from the media. They executed an examination of my daughter, Allison, and my sister, Lisa Marie. Through facial recognition and the latest DNA technology, which has been proven to be 99.6 percent accuracy, the media lady came back to me and stated that, not only are we related, but in our resemblance, we could be twins. I proceeded to ask her if she could publish this finding. The reporter said that if she were to do that, being that my family was so powerful, that her career would be over. Which further explains why no media has ever published that I am not a fake. In addition to this, they have also never published any elaborate story in the press either because the simple truth is that this is no elaborate story. This is just the simple truth.

Now, so far, just nonbelievers can still say that this is all rubbish. I, myself, even with full government approval, have not seen my complete DNA results. I needed to see them. I needed them on file. I needed the results to be in a form that could never be altered, so no one could say that they had been tampered with. I also needed family to have access to the results. Thus, I set off on a mission to accomplish this for "you," anyone out there. This became a very important mission for me, as I understand that many people in the public may need absolute evidence that "You are you," and that is all there is to it.

ULTIMATE EVIDENCE

We need to start out with the fact that I was born in the United Kingdom. As far as anyone knew, my mother, Mildred, and father, Dennis, were English. English heritage goes way back and my parents were one hundred percent English, unlike in America, where there is a big mix of lineage. Many English people have pure breeding. My parents were both an army and farm family. They served in the first and second world wars, serving England in the army. They traveled to and from places like Germany and Iraq. They are a strong family of army heroes. If Dennis had been my real father, I would have been proud to follow in the family footsteps. There was undoubtedly something that was kept out of the picture regarding my life. For such a long and tormenting time, I did not know what it was. I cannot put into words how lost I felt. It was truly horrendous.

Thus, as noted, I was supposed to be one hundred percent English. This would mean that considering my DNA, all of my relatives would be in England. There would be no way that I would have any element of America or any other country in my DNA. But, the father that is my rightful father, Elvis Presley, is in big part English and European. Many people who were born in America who have English ascendants can obviously have a very high percentage of English DNA. My DNA, firstly, rules out the father, Dennis, that I grew up with.

My DNA positively shows that Dennis Charles Mower was not my real blood father. In fact, there is no trace whatsoever to his heritage in my DNA.

Herewith, we are going to explore who my natural father is, in true knowledge of my assertion that it is Elvis. My DNA tests show that I am English, Scottish, Welsh, Irish, European (German, French, etc.), American, Cherokee, and Melungeon. I have all of the markers in my DNA, and the same Y DNA that my father, Elvis, has. Even though I was born in England during the army's activities, many of my relatives show up as being in America with the same mix of DNA spread throughout the world, with my first three cousins related to the Smith, and/or Adkins family, from Tennessee.

When a DNA test is run, a surname is not used. Rather, they take one's raw DNA and enter it into international data bases. That then starts the ball rolling in attaching surnames based on DNA evidence. If the first father, Mower, had been my real father, then he and other names connected to Mower would show up. But in my case, overwhelmingly it showed up as Smith, Presley, Wallace, White, and all of the other related family surnames stretching through time. My DNA heavily places me in Virginia, North Carolina, Mississippi, and Tennessee. Of course, there was still the evidence of English and European heritage stretching through European countries out to India and into West Africa. It is the western European heritage and connection to the Adkins family that makes the Presley's to be Melungeon, and it is the

White family, southeastern rare B DNA heritage that makes us Cherokee.

Elvis Presley's DNA was run a couple of times when he was living, and later. In the course of time, it became confusing to know whether that DNA was real or fake, as some of the findings had become tainted. However, Elvis's original Y DNA, Haplogroup evidence published online by historians and my DNA are a match and contains a rare B gene. It is undeniable that my DNA is on both sides of Elvis Presley's family, making Elvis and me related. Taking in all of this clear evidence and considering the fact that I am so much like my father in so many ways, and the certainty that my DNA places me smack in the middle of both sides of the Presley family, as previously explained, as well as Mississippi and Tennessee through DNA, and relatives DNA, it is pretty genuine and unmistakable about who I am.

With the new DNA technology today, anyone can see who they are in doing a fair amount of research, locating relatives and locations. It is not a mystery anymore, just simply hard DNA facts.

But, just in case there are still any doubters, the public needs to know that my DNA was analyzed by the world's top DNA scientists, placed in the world's largest and most advanced DNA matching system, and stored in The University of Arizona's medical research university.

My final DNA narrows me down to settling in Tennessee, with the possibility of just two hundred fathers. Since my DNA markers, and Y

DNA match Elvis Presley, plus with all of the other evidence combined, Elvis is my father within a factor of billions to one. DNA of my father came from very reliable official sources, connecting both sides of the family's DNA.

HERE ARE MY DNA FACTS:

Within DNA, there are two ways to determine paternity. The first and most common are when the father and child are still living. The DNA samples of both parties are sent to the lab and the lab sends a letter back showing the paternity results. The second method, in the case when the father is deceased, is to take the child's DNA along with the father's relative's DNA, in putting together a DNA family tree.

Luckily for me, DNA science historians have published Elvis Presley's DNA on the internet. Altogether, the DNA matches me, along with cousins who have available DNA on both sides of the Smith and Presley families.

Furthermore, I was born in the United Kingdom. A part of my DNA places me in Tennessee with some of my closest cousins, including X match cousins, who are also from Tennessee. In fact, out of 1707 matches of mine, they all connect, either way, on both sides of the Smith and Presley families.

MY BIRTH CERTIFICATE

Details of my birth certificate are as follows:

David Mower does not exist. The reason for that is that all of the records for David Mower have been sealed or deleted by the American and British governments. This was executed due to a court order based on decisions made by the court which changed all of my legal and medical records in both the United Kingdom and United States to Elaine Elizabeth Presley.

My birth certificate reflects that I am a female, Elaine Elizabeth, born in Clacton On the Sea, Essex, England.

In 2018, a further order was placed, based on 2017 DNA evidence that Dennis Mower is not the biological father of me, Elaine Elizabeth Presley, formerly David Mower. This action removes him and adds the correct parental information, as it is now known to be Elvis Aaron Presley.

A CHILD OF A LEGEND'S REALITY

One would think, as millions do, that in being related to a legend, one's life is simply and completely filled with an entitled and privileged existence with unlimited money and endless partying. I am awarded more than most people do receive. People out there look up to me and admire me for who I am. My job, in exchange, is to act accordingly to family and society rules in order to continue my legacy correctly for the public. This is a huge responsibility and it is interesting that my original thoughts were to be a regular person in regular clothes supporting people.

I later realized that because people look up to me, the public does not want to see me hanging around out there trying to be like everyone else because I am not like everyone else. They want to see the full blown branding of who I am within my legacy. I was trying to give the public my respect by trying to maintain my down-to-earth self. But, it does not work. I am out there in the world, as part of my legacy, and people surprise me all of the time with wanting hugs, photographs, autographs, etc. I am not an ordinary person. I am part of a legacy and I have to live up to my role within my family. There could be a tremendous downfall and massive backlash for me if I could not do just that.

Being who I am really hit home to me when I thought that I could go out and apply for a job to earn extra income in order to build my career faster. I was hard hit with my circumstances. Being who I am with my fame can create problems for companies who are interested in hiring me. A simple job interview can become more like a celebrity "meet and greet." Organizations that are not used to hiring celebrities can become overwhelmed in that I even applied. In addition to this, I am not just representing the company. I am also maintaining the image of my family legacy. Whether I am working for an organization or attending a hit Broadway show, my presence could be taken as an endorsement. These examples, as such, have to be correctly licensed and paid for, which comes under our legacy management for image and branding.

So, as you can see, I cannot just do anything I want because everything has its rewards and consequences. Everything must be by contract and approved because I am representing our family. At this point, my responsibilities hit me hard. I then immediately, upon recognizing this reality, upgraded my attitude and my image to the high level that the public, along with my legacy demands of me. From that place, I continue my legacy. I have gotten my act together and I focus just on my family, company, foundation, and career within Graceland. I have been smacked in the face and smacked into shape.

You may be wondering, "How can you possibly do that? Isn't it impossible to go from trying to live a normal life to all of this big stuff?" My answer is simple and direct. "No, that's my job. That's what I do. That is my role and my position; to live up to our legacy and to continue it." This should give you an insight of what celebrities have to deal with on a daily basis. We do things that are hard. We make things happen from nothing, and we create. On the other hand, being me is not all that simple. Many times I have to go out and have to cope with being recognized and always acting in accordance with protection of our legacy, along with treating the public with the utmost respect. I have to represent my role within my legacy continuously, at the highest level, 24/7, 365 days a year. It does not matter if I am tired or not, I still have to live up to my role.

In addition to all of this, there is the subject of money. Since I am in a famous family, it seems like everybody is scheming to get my money. Then one must understand that we are controlled by rules, companies, managers, advisers, etc. Most importantly, at the time of this book's publication, I do not receive a large allowance from my upbringing. I, as a famous kid, am subject to amazing pressure. Being freshly home in my family, I have to learn how to negotiate as far as what I want. Nobody just hands me a load of money. I quickly found out that I am dealing with a powerful bunch of management executives that I may have to potentially sue and/or make deals with that are good for me. If I make a bad deal, these executives would have me pinned to the wall. It is not a "lovey-dovey" situation. It is a ruthless and emotionless business environment.

When I first arrived home with who I am, with a big smile and wanting to love the world, I found out within the first four years, I was slaughtered. I am responsible for being strong and making my own accurate business decisions. Being a celebrity child, I am not always wanted. I can be seen as a risk, a threat, or an asset to the management team. Nobody is going to hold my hand. I have to stand on my own two feet with the gifted talent that God and my father bestowed upon me, and thereby make a successful life for myself within my family."

THE HEART OF THE MATTER

In this important segment, I desire to inform and elaborate so that the reader can better understand the truth and facts and myths behind gender identity disorder (GID), also known as Gender Dysphoria.

Most people think that there are two genders; male and female. This would actually be correct. However, it is not all black and white. There is a big grey area where things can get mixed up at birth. We have all seen men who are very effeminate, and we have seen women who are very manly. Now, both of these "grey area" people have the correct brain for their individual sex. The effeminate man is actually a man with a man brain. The butch woman is actually a woman with a female brain. There are essentially no issues or problems with them because they have no desire to change. They are "grey area" people who are content with who they are. The challenge arises when you tip the balance and place a female brain in the male or a male brain in a woman. This marks the entrance into the world of the transgender.

Until recently, there really was no science to verify and understand these "mixups." The system of knowledge is much more clear now as to know whether one is supposed to be a girl or a boy, regardless of what genitals one may have been born with. There are advanced developments that can pinpoint exactly what kind of brain a child has, so that ultimately that uniquely different kid does not have to grow up dealing with and struggling with gender issues all of his or her life. In having the correct brain for the correct body, a person has harmony. Everything in the body must be aligned. The mind must work together with the heart and soul, the body makeup and the gender. It all works in unison and, if one of these aspects is off, it can have devastating consequences.

Medical technology also has the ability now to understand how and why some sexual parts are mixed as both male and female. This offers a unique opportunity for parents with children who have gender dysphoria to keep a watch over them in eliminating the misfortune of these offspring growing up and having to hide their feelings and true selves in a gender that they do not feel comfortable in. Therefore, the hopeful goal would be to set in motion, a way to fix the situation at an early age of possibly somewhere between five and ten years old.

In fact, this was within the age bracket that I (then David) was evaluated by doctors, and they first deciphered that I needed some form of corrective surgery. At that time, the science did not exist to determine the correct sex. The questions used in trying to determine the right gender were along the lines of, "Do you want to play football?" Even though I hated football, I was told to say that I liked it. This sadly resulted in spending many months in the hospital to make me more of a complete boy. Dismally, no one understood the realization that I had the female makeup in my brain, except for my mom and grandma.

In recognition of fairness to the doctor, I could see on his face that he was unsure if he was making the right decision for me. The doctor, in respect to also being fair, then told me that he could wait until later on to make up his mind about the proper choice. The doctor informed me that by my not having this corrective surgery at that time, there would be a higher risk of getting cancer, being that my body had elements of both genders.

I was scared of this "false" father, Dennis, that was with me. I was embarrassed to tell Dennis that I needed to be a girl, since Dennis was a hardened army hero and a farmer/logger. Dennis had improperly pressured me to tell the doctor that I loved playing football and boy games, with the intention of later getting rid of me by making me enlist in the army. So, I did what I was told. On top of that unbearable constraint, I was never given a proper explanation of what kind of operation I was going to receive. All I knew was that I felt like a girl and I was too scared to talk about it.

In reflection, I feel that the doctor seemed to have a natural understanding more about these complex gender issues at a time when the science was not there.

I had been going to church on my own since early childhood and I loved God. I know that God made us all the way we are for His own good reason, and that He loves us all. Herewith, I wholeheartedly convey to you, any reader out there who suffers from any kind of gender disorder, "Do not, for one second, listen or buy into anyone that says that God hates you because of your gender dysphoria. This is simply not true!"

As you have learned, my gender issues occurred at birth. What is compelling is that, if that doctor had made me female in that early surgery, then no one would be saying anything. But, because I had to suffer for many years in different genders, it opened the doors to a lot of controversy. Yet, the plain facts are that I was really a female all along. Due to lack of science and a controlling stepfather, I was made to be male on the outside. Henceforth, after many years living inside the wrong gender, I was able, with the help of the new department of learning, to finally live and to be who I really was as a woman.

Accurately, I did not suffer from any kind of mental problems, apart from the fact that I had to painfully handle being in the wrong gender for such an extensive time. Nonetheless, after the final correction of this quandary, I now live a regular and fulfilling life as a female. I am truly not transgendered. This is backed-up through thorough medical examinations by doctors and psychiatrists. In fact, the very last words that the physician said to me upon completion of my transition, "This file is closed, and there is no reason for you to come back. So, get out there, live your life and be happy!" I relive so vividly my recollection after that last appointment as I was skipping down the street, feeling very elated and happy and saying to myself, "Well, that's it, I'm done!" There is no doubt that I was always a female who had former medical issues. I am one of the lucky ones and have been able to undergo a completely normal life as a female.

REFLECTION OF MY DAUGHTER

As previously stated, Allison blossomed into being a very wholesome, mature, and well-rounded young lady. She is very intelligent. She became a successful model. She graduated from college as a skin specialist. She also owned several successful businesses; a beauty care business, a legal services business, and health products business. In Miami, Allison ran a top beauty and skin salon with luxury yacht services. She appeared as a main actress in "Miami Nights". She was a sophisticated host and now lives with her husband along with my two handsome grandsons and one beautiful granddaughter.

In retrospect, my daughter and I went through a lot during my divorce from her mother. Plus, we moved around quite a lot. We actually had a lot of fun mixed with sad times. I feel that this is a common fact among many divorced parents with children.

There were many little times that Allison and I both remember, in the old days of selling signs. One in particular, and on a humorous note, was when we stopped off at a roadside café and we both agreed on ordering the soft crab sandwich. When the order was brought to the car, we opened up the wrapping and the sandwich had the crab in it, but the legs were hanging out. So, in holding our sandwiches in our shaky hands, we both looked at each other and started screaming and laughing. Then, in simultaneous stupor, we said, "What the heck?" In daring each other, together, at the same time, we plopped the sandwiches in our wary mouths. In two little crunches and two big shrieks, the sandwiches went out the window as the foot went on the accelerator and the car went skidding out of the parking lot, but not without Allison and me bellowing out, "That's disgusting."

I remember telling Allison, after we drove down the street, that in light of this experience, "You better do well in school, otherwise you'll be going down the road selling signs, like this, for the rest of your life."

Another funny time that I recall with Allison was when we were in the food court of the mall in Virginia Beach. Allison was about five years old. I was having curried snacks, and Allison was eating chicken nuggets. I looked at her and said, "These are really hot." She asked to try one. I said, "Okay, I'll give you a bet. If you can eat one of these, I'll give you five dollars." No sooner than that was said, Allison gulped it down, and then she put her hand out and gave me, what is now known to be the "Presley look," and said, "Five dollars." Of course, I gave it to her.

Allison and I had, and still have, a very close relationship. We had so many wonderful fun times, full of excitement and education. Allison was very lucky because, even though I took care of many job situations, I was mainly self-employed, working only about two hours a day while Allison was at school. She never ever really saw me work, other than in the early days, selling signs. I used to get up in the morning, fix breakfast, travel to school with Allison, give her lunch money, pick her up, cook dinner, stay on top of her doing homework, occasionally take her to movies or shopping in the mall.

We also used to watch movies at home, chat, laugh, and play games like Monopoly. We loved an old English card game named "Snap." I used to make sure that she got ready for bed on time. I read her made-up bedtime stories that were often wild and crazy. Then, I kissed her on the cheek or forehead saying, "Goodnight, see you in the morning and I love you!"

In order to help Allison sleep, and to live a comfortable, happy life, I decorated her room however she wanted it. I surprised her with life-like stars and the moon on the ceiling with shooting stars. Thus, when I turned out the light, instead of being in darkness, her whole ceiling opened up into a midnight sky. This would allow her to fall asleep within a few minutes. My daughter had a nice life with trips to Disney World, playing with friends, going to theme parks, shopping, going to movies, and eating out with a solid, supportive home life.

On weekends, we used to travel to neighborhoods looking for our dream home; that big white house with the lions and an electric gate. I never really found my dream home back then. Now, I know that the home I was searching for was my family home, located at 3764 Elvis Presley Blvd, Memphis, TN 38116, USA. I finally found "home" on May 6, 2013. I feel like my Dad wanted me to live my life first, then "come home" later.

Enter Elvis

All throughout my ascending life, the Elvis factor, in pure essence of true reality and supreme spirit was always there; surrounding, watching over, guiding, and saving me. Regardless of the fact that for so many years, this truth of Elvis Presley being my father was hidden and "hushed up," I subconsciously "knew" all along, and my soul would take me on an evolving and culminating path.

Overall, regarding the facts about Elvis and me, many exact details remain hidden; whether or not I was conceived in Germany or England.

I feel in my heart that Elvis would today be with Priscilla, or at least be best friends with her. He loved all the women he dated, but they were bandages hiding from his true love, Priscilla.

No doubt, as already relayed, the moving phone call from me, the young teenager to Elvis, speaks for itself in meaning and impact. Those poignant words from Elvis to me say it all, "Just live your life and be happy. I will be there for you when you need me."

Then, of course, the remarkable illuminating reawakening for me in 2013 is when I had the strong spiritual connection with my father and realized that I was indeed Elvis' child. The one thing the world needs to understand is that Elvis Presley continues to be here for me to this day.

It becomes more and more evident that Elvis left Lisa and me a distinctive road map to follow, as guidance within our lives. Here is one out of hundreds of things I have learned and continue to learn from my father.

My father taught me, "If you have fame and wealth without happiness, what do you have?" I believe the same as my father. I like the level of fame that I have earned, just enough to live a life of happiness without the pressure. Health, Family, Self, and Happiness are all we need. I am following our family road map.

REFLECTION OF MY MOTHER

My mother's favorite song was "Green, Green Grass of Home."

I have two distinct memories as a baby. People say that one's memory does not go back that far, but I remember it so well, and I know it to be true. When I checked into this matter, I found out that you can indeed have vivid memories going back to early childhood, especially when there is a shocking impression.

There are two main occasions, as a little child. The first, is being at Nanna's house in the pram, by the piano in a room opposite from the living room. This was in a very small cottage where my grandmother, Nanna, lived. I can still hear my mother, Mildred, and Nanna talking, minute-by-minute, laughing, having fun, and the television being on. I wanted to be in the other room with them. I used to cry a lot.

I remember many other times, growing up, being at Nanna's. We used to visit her quite often. She was very loving and caring, and so was my mother. You had to be careful coming in the front door. It was slippery when it rained. I remember it splashing on my Wellington boots. I remember just down from her cottage, there was a gate with an arching roof on top. I remember Jack and me climbing up the gate, inside the little roof. We used to play there a lot and we wrote our initials in there. We used to walk the lanes and pick apples, pears, and blackberries.

This is where I spent the most wonderful time of my childhood. Growing up, I remember being hyper, sensitive, quiet, shy, and noisy. Nanna used to sit with me and talk with me. Nanna said, "Your dad played the piano, and you are a very special child. Your mum had a chance to be with another man, but she didn't do it. I was upset with that decision. You need to remember always that you are from somebody very special."

The other main occasion, in remembrance as a baby child, is this highly treasured and emotional moment.

I remember meeting my real father when my mother, Mildred, took me to see him. He gave me a brown teddy bear with a moving head, arms, and legs. I loved my teddy throughout my childhood. When I met this man, I was just a baby, but I remember him crying, like he wanted to take me. My mother was very protective of me and became nervous and said she had to go.

This is the only time I ever met this man whom I now know to be my father, Elvis Presley. My mother was very loving and protective of me. I was her favorite. She looked after me very well and did everything she could do and more. Dennis, on the other hand, was vicious and verbally violent to me. One time, I remember getting into the car to go to Nanna's, and Dennis looked at me through the car window and said, "Get the hell out of here, you little bastard!"

Dennis made it clear that he was not my father and he mentioned it a few times. I thought he was my father, as I did not know any differently.

REFLECTION OF MY PAST MARRIAGE

From the time I met Desiree, it was always a challenge because I suffered from gender problems and was very female within myself. I realize now that I had more of a female brain than a male brain, and Desiree and I were more like sisters. Of course, we shared a marital bed, and she was a very beautiful woman. I felt she was happy with our love life. However, I was never a "manly guy" and I sensed she was psychologically searching for that.

My focus was always on my wife and daughter. I was not, however, that full man that most women seek. I was more of a mother to Allison, and I still am to this day. I tried to be a man, but it was not natural for me. My male friends did not like to go out with me when they had a "guys night out" because they felt like I was not really "guy-like and tough enough!"

I quite sadly believe that most of the trouble in our marriage was related to my gender issues. Romantic life was good, as I could feel what she wanted, but I just did not have that manly feel that many women seek.

Desiree and I ultimately filed for separation, and we agreed on joint custody of Allison. Raising my daughter, Allison, was the most beautiful experience of my life.

Later on, Desiree found the right partner. She has now been happily married for many years. We remain friends to this day.

DISCOVERIES

I came to the realization that the custom home I grew up in, that was built for my family, may not have been given by the farmer. In real facts, farmers did not build homes for laborers in England because poor families like mine were given English Council Housing with rent subsidies by the government. There was no one else at that time that was given a free house for working on a farm, and the home was totally free. It is still in the family today, long after Dennis passed away.

In the beginning, I believed our home was given to us by the farmer. It becomes evident that it was more likely paid for by Elvis Presley, but I do not know that to be one hundred percent true. It is just a feeling that I have deep in my heart.

Recently, it was comforting and rewarding for me to receive this major letter of recognition on July 12, 2018 from the Commander of the Elvis Presley Memorial Post.

ELVIS PRESLEY MEMORIAL POST 11333

2600 ELVIS PRESLEY BOULEVARD

MEMPHIS, TENNESSE 38106

July 12, 2018

To whom it may concern:

By the power vested in me as Commander of the Elvis Presley Memorial Post 11333 Memphis I hereby appoint Ms. Elaine Elizabeth Presley to the Building Committee of the Elvis Presley Memorial Post 11333 Memphis, Tennessee. Ms. Presley is an integral part of the renovation and rejuvenation of our post. Without her help our post would not have been able to maintain its beneficial presence in this community.

Her father, Elvis Aaron Presley, was a veteran serving in the United States Army Tank Corps in Germany. She is following in his foot steps as a proud supporter of American military servicemen and women.

Sincerely,

Eugene Kelly McDuffie, Commander
Elvis Presley Memorial Post 11333 Memphis

Most recently, I created and implemented the "Princes and Princesses Children's Charitable Program." The story behind this program derives from one beautiful Christmas day in 2016 at Graceland. I had just finished having dinner with my friend, Julian of Capitol Records, when I heard this call from across the room at the Graceland Guest House Hotel. "Hey, Ms. Presley, come on over and talk to us!" I looked at Julian and he looked at me. I smiled and said, "Let's just go with it."

It was a family from the United Kingdom, my fans. The first thing the gentleman, Jimmy, said to me was, "Are you okay, Ms. Presley? How are you within yourself?" This was a lovely comment that moved me. I replied, "I am doing fine. How are you?" They were all doing well, too.

They insisted that I sing them a song. So, I sang, "I Can't Stop Loving You", which was good because Julian later said that it was jaw dropping. He was so impressed that he gave me an open invitation at Capitol Records anytime. He even suggested that he would come down from California with his crew to record me in the Jungle Room, maybe on the following Christmas.

The following morning, I bumped into the same couple when they were getting ready to leave the guest house. I had time to get to know them a little bit better. First, I could not get out of my mind the remark that Jimmy asked me about if I was alright, and I thanked him for caring so much.

It turned out to be a great fan photo opportunity and I had the delight to meet their little girls. One was about two years old and had previously had brain surgery. I received permission to have her sit on my knee for which she had the biggest smile that lit up the room. Then, it became time for me to make my exit. I never had the chance to do something that I regret to this day. I wanted to give that precious little girl a teddy bear.

This has played on my mind over the last two years, and it was the basis of my designing the latest charitable program for the Elaine Elizabeth Presley Foundation at Graceland, called "Princes and Princesses Children's Charitable Program." The program works like this: every child from birth to nine years old who is unwell, living with a major illness who visits Graceland from the start of this program on December 24, 2018, will be eligible with a valid Graceland ticket to receive an Elaine Elizabeth Presley Foundation teddy bear.

One of the great benefits of "being home" at Graceland is that I get to design things for my family, proudly assisting our entire team, in continuing our legacy. Even though my road home gave me many challenges, it was also the most wonderful journey.

My successes so far over the past five years have proven that I can stand-up on my own two feet to represent Graceland. I have been grateful for several media credits, including radio, television, and stage.

I am proud that I have been behind important causes. I am an advocate for anti-bullying, and my charity, "Elaine Elizabeth Presley Foundation", which assists adults, children, and pets on a daily basis. I reinstated Rock N' Roll on June 15, 2013, by publishing a news release. I have attended major events for our family history, and I am thrilled that my sister and I have jointly created our Graceland Anthem, to be released soon.

In addition, I am pleased that I have contributed other designs, improvements and ideas for Graceland, of which some have been beneficially utilized. These include multi-currency on the Graceland website, photos of Elvis fans, the Graceland vacation layaway program, a camp where children can come to start their music careers, the Graceland rose garden, a kid's crafts and painting area, and a Thomas Kinkade, known as the "Painter of Light," master Graceland Christmas limited edition art to exhibit at Graceland.

I am happy to announce that the following is the latest concept for my Graceland team. My in-depth research shows that within 300 miles of Graceland, and, I'm sure beyond, we have the type of Elvis fan who has either visited Graceland before or has never done so, but desires to do so. The one amazing thing that I discovered is that the vast majority of these fans of all ages do not know about our latest improvements; the Guesthouse at Graceland, and our new entertainment complex.

I came up with the idea that we should extend our tour buses into tour coaches, picking up and returning home. The tour coaches should have movies and historical videos all about Elvis. This plan could increase our visitors from 600,000 a year to over a million.

I am grateful that people within my fan base have either already visited Graceland or are planning to take on this adventure.

I was invited to come down to Memphis and conduct a very important board meeting at Graceland with eight board members of the VFW Memorial Post 11333. I spearheaded this two hour productive meeting on November 3, 2018, in the country board room from 3:00 to 5:00 pm.

The meeting was highly successful and assisted in forging the future of Whitehaven, the community surrounding Graceland. My role as part of the estate is to merge the Elvis Presley name into an existing memorial post by re-naming it the "Elvis Presley Memorial Post 11333." The original Elvis Presley Memorial Post was formed in 1954 and continued until 2016 when it eventually closed. The post was then re-located from an industrial part of town into Whitehaven. There it sits now, reopened by the Commander, Eugene Kelly McDuffie, all of the board members, and by me, representing the Presley Family estate.

The plan is to continue the legacy of the Elvis Presley Memorial Post, while assisting veterans and the residents of Whitehaven. Also, it importantly includes improving the neighborhood and, thus, peoples' lives. This is indeed a moment in history, as I am at home, not only following the road map that my father left me, but helping enhance the whole district surrounding my family's home.

DNA

When I realized I was Elvis Presley's child back in 2013, I knew I had to run my DNA. I did this in 2017 and onwards. After I ran my DNA, it ruled out Dennis Mower and Mildred Hynard as my biological parents. Actually, the DNA testing revealed that Mildred Hynard, the woman that raised me, was my cousin. This discovery linked into my grandmother's side of the family, namely, Minnie Mae Hood.

I ran seven DNA tests; Living DNA, My Heritage, Ancestry, Family Tree DNA, 23 & Me, GED Match, and National Geographic. These are all linked to the world's largest family tree data bases Also, I went on national media and invited my entire family, Smith and Presley, to run their DNA against mine, for which many of them did, and the results came back positive. I have thousands of cousins all over the world connected to me by DNA that are also connected to Elvis and Priscilla.

When I first discovered through DNA testing that Elvis was my father, I had no idea that Priscilla was my mother. Priscilla's cousins reached out and informed me that Priscilla was my mother, and that they had actually been with her in Germany when she was pregnant with me. The information that Priscilla's cousins provided me with were later backed up by DNA, with multiple cousins, matching Priscilla as my mother. The family tree continues through the entire family, showing me as their child. No other parents show up in my DNA.

IMMIGRATION

I first arrived in America in 1984, in Norfolk, Virginia. I remained in the United States for many years. I returned to England after my daughter graduated from high school in 2003, in Roanoke, Virginia. On my return to America in 2015, I knew that I was Elvis Presley's child. I informed immigration of this news. Later on, I also informed them that Priscilla Presley was my mother the moment I found out.

This led to a seven year federal investigation. I endured twenty federal court appearances, DNA testing, biometrics, blood, urine, shots, physical and mental evaluations, and a whole range of interrogations. All of this was part of the process to legalize my status in determining who I am. Finally, in 2020, I was granted legal status as Elaine Elizabeth Presley, with Elvis and Priscilla as my biological parents. This ended any doubt legally of who my biological parents are. I live my life as me, because I know who I am now.

I AM ME

One of the amazing things that I experienced in being me is that people try to change me all of the time. They can see I am like my father and through whatever reasons that they have, they think that being like Elvis is exclusive to Elvis, and it is. We children, being like our father naturally, is not an act. It is who we are. I think maybe people get confused with tribute artists where people act to be like Elvis Presley. We have to remember that it is an act, and simply that, and not who they are naturally. We, the family, are like our father naturally in his traits, mannerisms, and looks. When people take a look at me, they do not want to believe that it is all real. They try to advise me to change or to be different so they can feel comfortable within themselves, thinking that what they try to do to me shows that I am no longer like my father. I am me. Everything about me is real. Being like my father is real. I just want people to understand this; that I am me.

I should have realized who I was earlier, really, as I was just like Elvis Presley. But I did not realize. The painful truth is I became lost after my father died in 1977. All the searching I was doing in trying to find myself, was because I was running away from my father's death. In all that I endured when, and after he died, I was simply running from myself, trying to find myself, and my heart and soul were knocking on my brain every second of the day, trying to tell me who I was. But my brain was on that fast moving train going in the opposite direction. I do know now that my "lostness" was a combination of my hard childhood with Dennis, the man who I thought was my real father, and the loss of my real father, whom I lost in 1977.

As a child, I was not allowed to have music lessons or sing. To my amazement, it still is exactly the same today. I have been successful since I have been home; singing, doing "meet and greets," recording, entertaining fans, and doing media interviews. All of it, except the things that are allowed, have been hidden, destroyed, or taken away.

Back in 2014, when I did a show in Wales, England, the existence of that show was made to disappear. When I danced and moved my hips like my father, proudly, just like Dad, I was banned from moving my hips in public, with a hard, firm message," That's one nail in your coffin, don't add anymore!"

So, as you can see, from childhood until now, I have been suppressed from singing, and I believe it is because I look and sound a lot like my father. Plus, after he died, it probably has something to do with the money, too. Regardless of what the reason is, up until now, I have been made invisible to the public eye.

When I came home, I thought the way I was doing things was right and I remained loyal. I have certainly learned a lot from my mother, as how to protect my intellectual property, create at a higher level, and run my part of being home like a business. Today, I do manage a small part of our estate.

I continued in 2018 to work for our family/legacy and to released my best new creative works to the world, which I certainly hope people will enjoy.

I have traveled a long way from looking over that bridge in Coggeshall, Essex, England when I projected that I belonged somewhere else. I searched on many roads along the way with many trials and tribulations. It was a long journey until that one day that a promise from my father finally came true. On May 6th, 2013, my father, Elvis Presley, brought me home.

I had to fight tooth and nail to seal and claim my place at home in Graceland. I have utilized my vision not only retaining my place, but building a successful debt-free foundation and company through it all. I am a prosperous business lady. I have proven to be a major asset to a legacy by already designing many things which move Graceland ahead into the future, and with many more ideas to come.

I am not a kid that grew up and came home to live off of my family. My dedication is to the ongoing support of Graceland. So, hand-in-hand with my sister, Lisa Marie, and my mother, Priscilla, and all of the children and grandchildren, I continue my life at home in Graceland on behalf of my father, Elvis, in heaven with God.

Some names in the book have been changed to protect their true identities.

"This book is the truth, the whole truth, and nothing but the truth, so help me, God!"

This is my entire life up until now. Let's see what happens next...

I am me.

The End

Printed in Great Britain
by Amazon

64385747R00160